Laundromat

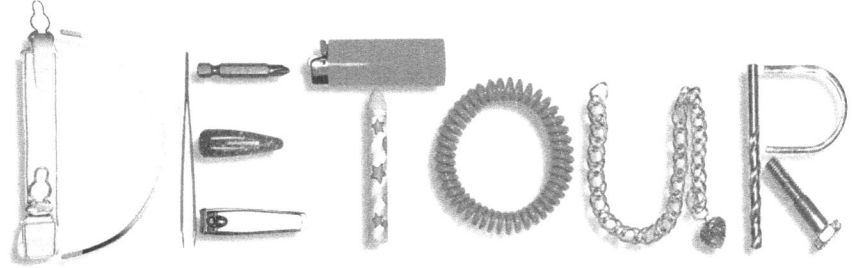

**Poems about
Liberated Bra Underwires
Quirky Customers
Mopping and More**

Leah M. Schulte

PUBLISHER'S NOTE: This is a work of creative non-fiction. Some parts have been fictionalized to varying degrees, for various purposes, with some names, dates, places, events, and details changed, invented and altered for literary effect, or to protect the privacy of the people involved.

Cover concept by Leah M. Schulte

Book layout and design, editing and cover art by Bob Zingmark

Photos from author's collection

ISBN: 979-8-9876828-0-7

First Edition: 2023

Independently published in U.S.A.

Authored by:

Leah M. Schulte

www.leahmschulte.com

email: leahmschultebooks@gmail.com

To all those who do laundry for others

TABLE OF CONTENTS

TABLE OF CONTENTS

Acknowledgments and Thanks

To:

My departed mother, for her lessons on kindness

My dad, for his lessons on work ethic and his capital support at our startup

Chris, an amazing business partner through roller coaster times

Kerry, for her steadfastness, social media prowess and more

Dan, for all his laundromat support and responses to our SOS texts

Mark, ever faithful cheerleader and attorney extraordinaire

The Wordsmiths at Washington Missouri's public library and writing group leader, Nelson Appell, who monthly, for years, critiqued yet another laundromat poem

Beta Readers Mary Edwards, Mike Ninness, Abby O'Rourke and Linda Hackmann who invested time and attention on the draft manuscript

Larry Godwin, departed creative writing mentor, and The Menagerie Group in Missoula, Montana

Bob Zingmark, for cover design, editing and formatting

Aaron Lelito, for developmental editing

Mike Borgerding, for brainstorming apparel export-import data

Joan Melcher, for inspiration, resources and MT recreation

Friends, family & strangers who gave feedback or at least didn't let their eyes glaze over when I mentioned this book again

Staff, current, past and future, who tolerate(d) my management angst and creative antics

Customers:

Moss, who consistently thanks us for keeping a clean laundromat

Tracy, who answers customers questions before we can assist

Paul, kind drop off customer, who always pays with $1 bills (since he knows we can use them) and exits with a "Get home safe tonight!"

Introduction

I never planned to own and operate a laundromat, aka mat. It was a detour on my life path. While paths for some people contain mostly straight sections, mine's been laden with cul-de-sacs, swinging rope bridges and roadblocks. So how, a laundromat? An older brother of mine in the industry repeatedly recommended the underappreciated coin laundromat as a solid business option. Then a younger brother, at a point in his aviation career, wanted to invest in a side business. And as I was weary and cynical of the healthcare industry and had relocated back to the Midwest to assist in the caregiving of my elderly parents, timing and opportunity aligned for a joint laundry enterprise. Hence, my brother Chris and I are co-owners of Midtown Washboard Laundromat in St. Charles, Missouri, a bustling city 30-minutes west of St. Louis. The electronic door to our mat opened on September 12, 2018.

This is not a typical book about laundry or laundromats. Expect no stories about bubbles, stain treatment, equipment repair tips or ROI figures. This is a collection of free verse poems about the mat and people that visit it, written with a personal and playful approach. Most were conceived from notes scribbled down in a little spiral notebook in my apron pocket as I folded wash, mopped and got to know customers.

The first two chapters describe the laundromat, highlighting some objects then physical tasks I do there. The middle part of the book portrays some memorable customers. I share some two-bit psychology in the chapter on how to deal with nonstop "talkers" that grace our business. Next is an unusual chapter covering the various and sundry objects, or detritus, left behind in washers and dryers and some fictional backstories I created about them. The final short chapter contains contemplations on America from the perspective of this novice business owner, who had to employ people, battle an everchanging pandemic, witness racism, examine my own relation to race, question and embrace so much more.

continued

Sprinkled about the book are photographs I've snapped, all with my cellphone. I hope they capture the spirit of our business. Other photos creatively feature our laundromat detritus.

The purpose of this book is two-fold. First, it was therapy for me. While I'd been an entrepreneur before, a brick-and-mortar business added a whole new dimension. These poems helped me organize my thoughts and emotions to make some sense of this endeavor. During my unorthodox detour, I tried to fully engage with customers, staff and objects and to appreciate those connections. Might as well enjoy the detour, right?

Secondly, I hope to entertain and perhaps poke readers to also connect and be aware of their own connections, whether working in a warehouse, fast food drive through, office, caregiving for a fellow human, Zooming at home or wherever. May you all recognize and savor those connections on the straight sections and detours in your own lives.

-Author

Chapter 1

The Laundromat
and Things Here

Every space we inhabit is shared with things, some with extreme significance in our daily lives. Others we may use regularly, but fade into the background of our awareness. As co-owner and operator, I've become very appreciative and aware of the things in this space that I see and use almost every day.

The Trio

The trio of washboards graces our front wall.
Bona fide relics and
the basis of our name.

A glass one, unearthed at a yard sale.

The trusty never rusty metal one,
bequeathed to me by a cousin from some ancestor.

A miniature "lingerie" model,
a dear aunt's unused wedding gift.

Initially I envisioned a wall full of washboards
to dazzle customers as they enter,
but learned their rediscovered popularity
as a musical instrument severely limits availability.

So, the trio is it.

I run my fingers across the zigzag ridges,
smoother on the glass, tighter on the mini,
and that sensation elicits visions of
bricks of harsh bar soap
tubs of cold water at awkward heights
rolled up sleeves
forward leaning positions combining body weight
    with elbow grease

and wonder,
what gave out first: washboard, fabric or skin?

Sacred Space

Engrained in our lives are sacred spaces:
childhood backyard
first apartment of liberation
home with loved ones we've chosen or created
car interior
workspace
beloved spots at a church, bar, library, gym.

Before it was our laundromat
this was a dime store with
cards and penny candy followed by a
local pharmacy which went belly up then
vacant for years as
national chains broke in.

I learn from an aged resident
someone committed suicide here
while it was a drug store.
She indicates the rear of the mat.
An overdose in the back pharmacy office?
Owner or staff?
What despair drove that act?

I start to search the internet for details
then stop, appalled.
I don't want to give more energy or
attention to the tragedy.

Is this space tainted?
That very spot scarred?
Do negative vibes persist?
Like the home of a murder or
hospital room seared into memory or
a stretch of highway marked with crosses?

But in a way,
the act of laundering here is a purification ceremony.

Dirt is overpowered by water and soap.
Bleach, laundromat incense, permeates.
Customers bend, reach, stoop and even
kneel in prayerful gyrations.
Revolving machines emit rhythmic incantations.

And the simultaneous:
watching TV
checking phones
snacking from a vending machine
playing with toys in the Kid's Corner
reading of People, a Bible or coupon flyers
and other seemingly mundane acts
add to the ritual.

I pray that the summation of the
everyday necessity and goodness of life
erases any aura of misery left here.

Today a laundromat.
After this, what?
May it remain a sacred space, always.

Majestic Machine

I use key RL003 to unlock then lift up your lid
and gaze down upon your innards marveling at your:
hoses and clamps
computer boards
wires
switches
belts
valves
coin drop
credit card reader gizmo
huge metal drum below
molded plastic soap dispenser above
and so much wizardry in between.

And it all works
usually.
Mostly always
actually.

It's not an MRI or supercomputer or nuclear centrifuge,
but I'm still impressed by this
Speed Queen washing machine.
My finger touches the start button,
water gushes, and 22 minutes later,
clean laundry emerges.

And behind all that gushing and whirring
I think of the brain power, human ingenuity
and muscle that contributed to
this majestic machine
here before me.

Encompassed in this seemingly inert appliance are
engineers' fingers clicking on a keyboard
designers sketching
CEOs analyzing figures
factory workers monitoring other machines which pound
    and shape metal
electricians threading and fastening wires like
    the nerves in our human bodies
crews in white lab coats and hair nets bent over
    conveyer belts of chips
a captain steering a ship of parts across the wide Pacific
forklift operators loading pallets of machines
    onto delivery trucks
sales reps expounding and pointing
and more.

And behind this machine's creation,
I acknowledge all the:
skipped coffee breaks
rushed deadlines
redone spreadsheets
botched prototypes
ditched marketing plans
nicked hands
strained backs
tired feet
missed dinners or soccer games or gymnastics meets

as again my finger stretches out to
operate it,
and I thank you all.

Tea Party Redux

The used plastic kitchen set
transports me back 50-plus years to
a time of simple pleasures,
uncomplicated desires,
and the power of pretending.
When a sturdy cardboard kitchen set
assembled by my father pre-Christmas Eve
and miniature accessories captivated me.
The Easy-Bake Oven was my next love,
but it all started with that kitchen set,
the first toy of my memory.
An onset of an era with a vocabulary including
Slinky, Etch A Sketch, Lincoln Logs and Barbie,
not Speed Queen washer extractors, OxiClean and
WaveBrake wringer mop buckets from my current world.

I accept the invitation from myself
and sit cross-legged on the gray floor mat
in our Kid's Corner
sandwiched between the kitchen on the right and the
mini talking tool bench and a
vintage washer-dryer combo unit, from eBay, on the left.

The teapot is missing a lid.
The pink teacups are saucer-less.
The spoon I stir with is from a different utensil set and
barely fits in the cup.

It is out of scale, like me.

Nevertheless,
I extend my pinkie,
now a longer, crooked, speckled one,
and lift the micro cup to my lips.

Mmmm.

We and HGTV

It's tricky,
finding a TV channel with broad appeal.
The news is O-U-T of the question.
The weather gets monotonous.
Cooking shows promote hunger pangs.
So my top choice is HGTV,
to carry me through my workday chores.
Some regulars even request this channel,
grab a snack and pull up a chair.
Other customers who are drawn back into the
TV orbit at the rear of the mat become converts.
Together,
we partake in these housing hijinks.

We watch Chip and Jo's
miraculous makeovers and marvel at
their growing offspring: kids, Magnolia, magazines, food.
Fixer Uppers of homes and more.

We witness Tarek and Christine
bicker and banter and beautify homes in
Flip or Flop (rarely) in
sunny southern California.

We smile back at the dimpled charming Property Brothers
and struggle to tell these identical twins apart.

I scrutinize the interactions of
another renovating sibling duo,
Leanne and Steve Ford,
since I am in business with my brother also.

House of Cards

continued

19

Loving wins over leaving
in the playful dueling between Hillary and David
on Love It or List It.

Gradually, we learn the lingo:
open concept kitchen
master ensuite
shiplap
subway tile
waterfall edges

We gawk at couples' quandary over beach front estates,
bemoan millennials' choices for foreign apartments
and raise eyebrows over lottery winners' new digs.
From Indiana to Mississippi to Hawaii
we endure sticker shock, rapid rehabs and
breath-taking décor.

Luckily, our customers are usually gone after 1.5 episodes.

Though some customers have broken laundry appliances,
most are renters and own none.
From this fantasy world on HGTV
I pray when they return to their washer- and dryerless
residences,
that they caress their nicked-up Formica counters tops,
praise their particle board cabinetry,
admire their low-grade plumbing fixtures and
adore their inadequate lighting.

May they give thanks for their genuine, familiar,
comfortable abodes.
While it's likely not their forever home,
I hope we can be their forever laundromat.

Cameras for Security and More

Clueless or careless,
You are captured
on our eight security cameras
like on Candid Camera.

The sign
"Smile you are on our Video Camera"
bears the iconic yellow smiley face.

From the office or my cell phone
anywhere
I watch you:

overstuff the machine
spill laundry detergent on the top and down the front
    of the washer
talk and talk and talk on your phone
get so absorbed in a video on your device you forget
    about your laundry
enjoy your book
thumb through our magazines
work on a crossword puzzle
steal a roll of our paper towels, soap pump or Lysol spray
knit
clip your fingernails and sometimes toenails
practice your boxing moves in the glass reflection
    of our one-way mirror

continued

study at our desks in the corner
watch your kids climb into or push laundry carts around
    like bumper cars
read one of our storybooks to your kids
help a confused customer before the attendant can
rifle through the lost and found bin
go to the bathroom three times
play a Scratcher's lottery card and leave
    rubbings everywhere
bring trash in from your car
refuse temptation, then succumb to our vending
    machine snacks
wolf down your take-out meal
scatter dryer sheets on the floor
cram dry laundry into your baskets and dart off
lovingly fold and stack your garments in organized piles

I'm a business owner protecting my assets.
But am I also a spy,
a voyeur,
an armchair human behavior analyst?

And I ponder,
if you really knew
I was watching you,
would you act differently?

Grandma's Rinse Tub

What once removed dirt
now holds dirt.

What would Grandma think?

The deep scarred aluminum tub
on spindly legs with tiny wheels
is now a planter
by the front door of our laundromat.
It's home to a mini cactus garden with
colorful gravel and little signs.

I told customers it was
my grandmother's wash tub
but my aunt clarified
it was one of her two rinse tubs.

In the 40's and 50's
before her first automatic washer,
in her housedress, stockings and galoshes over low heels
Grandma descended the basement steps
to tackle the laundry for her family of six.

Monday was Wash Day.

She would:
turn on the electric washer (single lever, single speed)
let the clothes agitate in soapy water
wring the soapy clothes using the attached manual wringer
soak the items in the first rinse tub
wring them again
soak them in the second rinse tub
do a final wring
then hang them up on lines in the basement or outdoors
    based on weather.

continued

Water was everywhere my aunt described.

How many times did she dip her hands down
into this tub or its twin or its agitating cousin?
What did she think about during all that dunking
and splashing?

Maybe she:
worked out the week's meal plan
savored a child's or spouse's tender moment
solved a discipline issue
prayed
compared her current life to that on the farm of her youth
daydreamed.

Did she rinse away her worries, her pain, her frustrations,
this gentle unassuming woman
who lost a
father to suicide in the Depression
firstborn child to scarlet fever
husband to a tragic car accident
son to an overdose
breast to cancer?

Despite aching back and chapped knuckles,
this weekly chore yielded contemplation and satisfaction.
Transformed, may Grandma's rinse tub
be therapy for me too.

Numbers

Numbers tumble through my brain.
Some come out easily
like no-wrinkle permanent press shirts.
Others are cantankerous
like an emerging load of aprons with tightly twisted strings.

There is the:
computer user ID
not to be confused with the time clock log in code
safe combination code
interior and exterior door codes
passwords, alphanumeric, to all kinds of bank accounts,
    programs and files
target revenue goals
actual revenue analyzed in various time frames
target and actual number of machine turns (or uses) per day
prices entered in our register for drop off
    and senior discount rates
our loan interest rate
the # of payments left in our loan (gulp!)
our averaged gas, electric and water bills
the # of minutes for wash cycles based on temp
    and wash upgrades
the # of minutes in a full dryer cycle vs. topped off
    with a quarter
electronic door timer and light timer settings
temperature schedules saved on our thermostat app
the daily # of customers
the # of times I smiled minus the # of times I frowned
    (or worse) at customers
the grand total of times I doubted this business decision
the # of times I gave thanks for this endeavor (insufficient)

Laundromat Library

Our bookshelves
are really just two wide windowsills
in the front corner
behind the chairs
by some potted plants.
Kids' books on the right
grown up stuff 90 degrees to the left.

Most kids prefer
to play on their parents' cell phones
though some tear through the 3 foot horizontal stack,
look at covers and leave a mess.
But a few outliers, future visionaries,
will hunt Waldo,
rediscover fairy tales,
share an escapade with Scooby Doo,
soar into stars, poetry or
some new realm
from the books discarded, donated or purchased
for $1/bag from the local thrift store.

Most adults prefer their phones too,
our limited TV,
or a quick smoke outside
compared to our meager literary offerings
(there is a library branch across the street after all).
Some do peruse local newspapers,
magazines, self-help books or
Bibles that perpetually get stolen
then replaced via the same thrift store.

Nevertheless,
underappreciated.

If we could afford it,
adding heated leather lounge chairs or
fuzzy bean bag chairs,
muted lighting
and soft music might change that.

Lost and Found

Marked "THIS WEEK'S" and "LAST WEEK'S"
the contents grow and shrink and shift and
get scattered about on the floor.

Since the forlorn laundry baskets were stolen,
our lost and found items
now reside in twin cardboard boxes.

Washcloths
undies of all sizes and styles
hankies
bras, camisoles and tank tops
t-shirts
bath towels or pillowcases
masks and more.
But the sock reigns supreme.
All varieties: teeny baby socks, anklets, men's dress,
    men's work, hospital slipper socks.

Overlooked in washer drums after the spin.
Dropped on the floor.
Dangled to air dry from a cart rack.
Trapped in the cart frame.

They are joined by bigger items left behind
on folding tables or tops of washers,
be it jackets, caps, belts or stuffed animals.
Sometimes we must bag up a full load of clothes,
mysteriously abandoned,
and plop it down next to the overflowing boxes.
All together, they wait. Hopefully. Expectantly.

Our lost and found is democratic.

continued

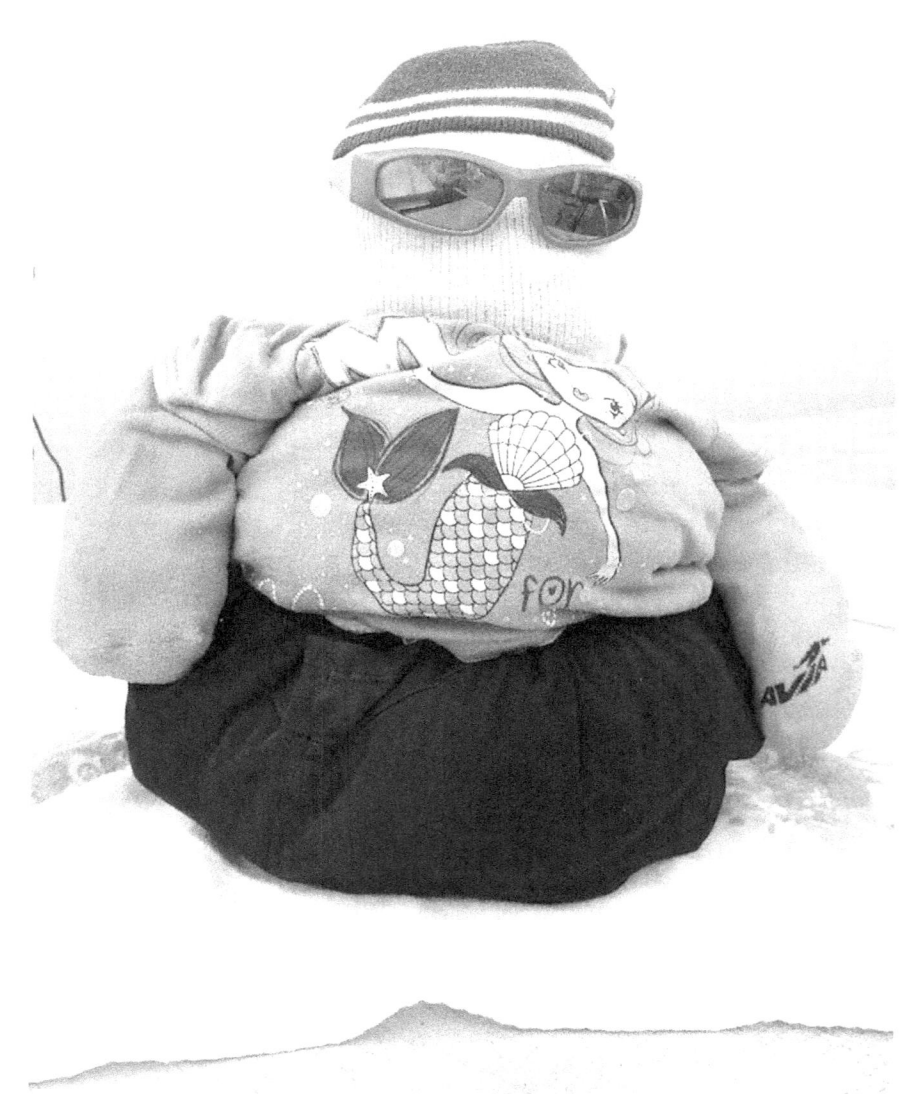

Lost and Found Snowman

Same for the hands that paw through it.
Our regulars on determined missions.
The homeless who have discovered it.
An attendant on a scavenger hunt
when a flustered customer phones.

But like on the Island of Misfit Toys,
(before Santa's arrival) most items remain,
forgotten
dispensable
unloved.

A few weeks later (since we are lenient),
the towels and washcloths enlarge our essential rag pile.
In upcycling attempts
linens might get sewn into masks and
old t-shirts woven into rag rugs.
And confession,
nicer items get snatched by staff
before the salvageable stuff is taken to Goodwill.

But best of all,
some socks are given a second chance,
a new lease on life,
transformed into ornaments on our store Christmas tree,
used as stuffing in other decorations and
truly resurrected,
as flying ghosts complete with wobble eyes
strung up on fishline above foam tombstones
on our washers at Halloween.

An Ode to Tape [1]

Tape, tape
everywhere there's tape
holding stuff together here
giving things shape.
Please stick. Don't give up.
I need you, dear tape.

I see you in all directions
up close and far away.
From mat opening to close
I praise you through the day.
To plastic roll or fat dispenser
"Thank you" is what I say.

Why?
Because you:

affix to the front door our ever-changing store hours
and last load cut-off

secure warnings near the entrance about no guns or
smoking or loitering

help inform customers we have surveillance cameras and
that they use the machines at their own risk

attach flyers explaining our masking policy, CDC COVID
guidelines and paper towels, wipes and Lysol locations

fasten notices about our Lost and Found, recycling bins
and coin changer

adorn the cash register computer with reminders

join scraps of paper with important info to bags of laundry

NOTICES

CREDIT CARDS MUST BE TAPPED IF
WASHERS & DRYERS REQUIRE
(NO TAPPING/APPLE UP DOWN
PAY) DUE TO A SOFTWARE ISSUE
WE APOLOGIZE

DUE TO EXTREME PRODUCT
THICKNESS, COLD OR ALMOST
EMPTY JUG, THE BLUE DOWNY
SOFTENER IS NOT GETTING
RELEASED IN RINSE CYCLE AS TOO
THICK FOR MACHINE LINES, PLEASE
DILUTE/THIN, SWITCH BRANDS OF
SEE ATTENDANT: THANK YOU!

EASTER HOURS
Sunday Hours
EASTER SUNDAY

NY laundry hours
6 am to 10 pm

Drop off Service

NOTICE

DO NOT ABANDON
YOUR LAUNDRY

Unattended laundry will be
removed by staff so
machines can be available
for other customers.

AUTOMATIC
CAUTION
DOOR

ACTIVATE SWITCH
TO OPERATE

continued

33

compete with the stapler for connecting receipts to
    our paper ledger

adhere staff schedules, old greeting cards and baggies with
    employee's cash tips to vertical surfaces around the office

help display the dreaded "Help Wanted" sign on the front
    window or cursed "Out of Order" sign on a broken machine

And even as I scrape your not-so-invisible magic
off glass or drywall or whatever surface
I still sing your praises.

Tape, tape
everywhere there's tape
holding stuff together here
giving things shape.
Please stick. Don't give up.
I need you, dear tape.

[1] If you choose, the opening and closing stanzas can be sung to the tune of "Signs", a 1971 hit single by the Canadian Rock group The Five Man Electric Band, written by Les Emmerson, lead singer.

Voices from the Vending Machine

High fructose corn syrup…who cares? You deserve
  a refreshing Pepsi.

Pretzels always go great with a Coke.
Or Diet Coke, don't forget me.
Watch out for his Cheetos dust on your whites.
Watch your mouth little Fritos, you're no Big Dippers for sure.
How come you always get the center row?
I'm the #1 best seller…don't mess with me.
Skip the hike to the drinking fountain, cold water's right here.
Green tea helps fight cancer. Drink up folks.
Think protein, think jerky. Try a stick.
Peanuts and plain M&Ms, side by side? Give us a break.
Classic Lays rule, pick me.
What about Sour Cream flavor for a change?
Or BBQ for a little zing?
Chips are old school, go with Nachos.
Forget the bakery next door at the grocery store…
    …cookies right here.

Six round peanut butter crackers for 50¢, a bargain.
Some Starbursts will help you fold your clothes faster.
Or Skittles since there's lots to share.
Fake news: pork rinds are popular in this state, too.
You're expired. How embarrassing.
Peanuts matter.
Hey, all snacks matter!

Holy Laundry

Zen Buddhist saying:
"After enlightenment, the laundry."
Carry on and apply enlightenment to even the
mundane chores that comprise our lives.

Gandhi:
Hindu, lawyer, renowned activist
pared down his wardrobe
to a simple white cloth as he wizened and aged.
While imprisoned he did his own laundry
to give the dhobi, the laundry man, a break.
As his wife lay sick and dying,
he washed her soiled clothing.
His legacy is to simplify and that
a person's dignity is not defined
by their clothing or tasks.

The Old Testament:
46 verses about clean clothing
many with companion references to also cleaning oneself.
Clearly, ritual purification was a common theme.
Cleanliness is next to Godliness.

New Testament:
Nothing specific about laundry.
But Jesus did wash his buddies' feet
so I imagine he connected with that gradually soiled towel,
and the hands, that later would wash it, as he demonstrated
his selfless act of service.
Plus, he was known for talking to women at the local wells
where they probably didn't do their laundry (maybe
a local stream?).

but he was aware of them drawing water and other chores
and struggles,
being the empathetic man he was, and a carpenter himself.

But most revealing
is that JC instructs his disciples
(Mark 6:9, Matthew 10:10 and Luke 9:3)
to go and preach wearing sandals
but only one tunic.
Hence, travel light in order to focus on your true calling.
Perhaps also cultivating gratitude for that sole garment.

My take on clothes (even though it might drive me
out of business):
Have less.
Take care of them mindfully.
Don't let them burden you.

Laundromat Symphony

whirrp   emits the innards of the electronic front door as it opens and welcomes all

urrrph eep dooolph   awakens the cash register computer and peripherals

deet doot doot dat dot   retorts the safe to a poking finger on the keypad before granting access

ummph   belches the HVAC unit with a blast of air

ching ching ching ching   verifies the changer swapped quarters for an inserted $1 bill

ergk dung   barks the soap vending machine as it begrudgingly releases then drops a miniature box of soap or softener

bangh clunk   cries the slammed then latched washer door

clink clink clink   indicates that coins were dropped to start the machine versus a

zzzzzzip   when a credit card is swiped through a mounted card reader

beep beep beep   alerts along with a visual PUSH START message on the display panel that the washer is ready

pissssshhhh   squirts the water as it passes through the soap dispenser cup proceeding to a crescendo of

whoooouuuuUUU   as it rushes full force through and down into the drum meeting dirty clothes followed by

slosh slap splish splash   that broadcasts a wash cycle underway and an

eeerrrrrr   that identifies a high-speed spin extracting water

whirrr tush   exclaims the snack vending machine as the horizontal motor pushes a snack forward off the shelf then lands at opening below unlike the

uuuulll thud   that announces a soda can arrival as it rolls down the chute and smacks the padded cavern below

inngg   sings an empty soda can as it ricochets against another when tossed into recycling

thang   slams the lighter dryer door followed by a
whosh   as the vent flap opens and then a rumbling
mmmmm   as laundry tumbles and dries with occasional
tap, click, scrape   proclaims the buckles, buttons and wedged screws against the drum wall

chchewww   coughs the brakes of the trash truck from behind out our back door, followed by
engggg   as its metal arms lift our dumpster to consume the contents and a
uuddDD   as it crashes to the ground, empty

eet eet eet   squeaks cantankerous laundry cart wheels

thunk   signals the front door automatic lock engaged, place empty

silence,
or maybe not

Chapter 2

The Laundromat
and Tasks I Do

Owning and working in a laundromat includes a wide range of activities. There are management tasks including collecting quarters, and hiring/firing staff, as well as mundane but vital chores, like cleaning the machines, mopping and folding laundry.

Ironing

heat + steam + a little pressure = flattened wrinkle free fabric

I do it on a quote basis since it's really a money loser,
a 15-minute set up before the first pass of the iron
plus interruptions.
Inefficient.

Honestly, I enjoy ironing,
especially under more leisurely conditions at home.
The satisfaction of a job well done.
Instant visual proof.

But, back to the beginning.
With that first pass of the iron,
there is something akin felt while also:
starting the mixer in a big baking project
pressing the pedal on the sewing machine to start an outfit
addressing the first envelope for those snail mail holiday cards
even boarding a plane.

Maybe it's the sense of embarking.

On A Good Day

There are days, exceedingly rare, when:

the machines spin endlessly without breaking down
and we hit our revenue targets.
Our computer systems work flawlessly.
The vending machines get heavy usage
and it is a jam-free day for the descending snacks
and beverages.

Staff show up, better yet, on time
and are hardworking and pleasant.
There are no cranky customers.
The comment box doesn't have any humdingers in it.
We get a 5-star Google review, or two.

I don't have to resolve what to do
when the homeless come in to get warm,
use our restroom,
charge their cell phones or
dine at our indoor picnic tables.

All the children who come in with their parents
are well-behaved and quiet.
The Kid's Corner remains crumb, sticky-fingerprint
and puke-free.

No one has made a mess in the restroom.
There's no thick coating of pet hair to clean out of washers.
Everyone picks their dryer sheets up off the floor
and puts them in the trashcan.
There are no soggy bottom trash bags
which split open enroute to the dumpster.

The wash dry fold counter is busy.
The orders I launder
contain no new red t-shirts that'll bleed,
sequined-encrusted garments or mysterious stubborn stains.
The undies look unblemished.
I precisely time the wash and dry cycles with my other tasks.
Wrinkle-free items emerge from the dryer
plus all the socks pair-up.

There's enough time to chit-chat with customers.
I write a poem, or three, in the
little spiral notebook kept in my apron pocket.
I don't have to stay late.
All the potted plants are thriving.

On a good day,
I have no doubts that this business venture will soar and
carry me into anxiety-free and
financially secure retirement years.

Bring on those good days.

FlipFold Fun

Steps:
place t-shirt upside down on this segmented plastic frame
center garment
turn over longer bottom edge to the frame border
flip left panel over
flip right
flip up bottom panel
turn item over.
Result:
one crisply folded t-shirt about the size of a magazine.

Sheldon, Sheldon, Sheldon,
of TV's The Big Bang fame,
you introduced the world to this gadget
even though Penny was oblivious to it.

Sheldon, Sheldon, Sheldon,
your cosmic quirkiness and
wacky ways are welcome here.

I'd sanitize and let you borrow a FlipFold
but you'd probably feel more comfortable bringing your own.
We could flip and fold from adjacent tables,
compare fun facts,
exchange foibles on friends and family,
laugh and snicker as our towers of t-shirts grow.

I'm sure we could craft a Laundry-Life Reciprocating Theory
to explain their intersecting truths,
plus solve the Folding vs. Hanging Garment Conundrum.
Together we can study the Black Hole for Missing Socks and
devise the Principle for Perpetually Shrinking Panties.

Better yet,
like your episodes with Stephen Hawking or Neil or other
fellow geniuses,
I can invite Martha Stewart, Marie Kondo and our
"Planet Laundry" magazine's guru Wally, and we can debate
stain removal techniques,
soap-softener ratios,
laundry basket properties and
optimal underwear drawer organization.

What amazing gains to laundry science we'll make!

But honestly,
I'd be happy with just you.

Sheldon, Sheldon, Sheldon,
come flip and fold with me.

Be A Nice Human

THAT'S ALL YOU GOT?

Imagine pleasant nonsense

Make Progress or Make Excuses

BREAKING NEWS: nobody cares

REALITY CALLED and I hung up

I AM Like No Other

Broken Hearts Club

WHEN THIS VIRUS IS OVER I STILL WANT SOME OF
YOU TO STAY AWAY FROM ME

No Mistakes Just Happy Accidents

I BELONG IN A PARK

God. Goals. Grind.

STAYING POSITIVE that it will all go horribly wrong

DONT PANIC

Give this world GOOD ENERGY

Out of Order

MY BED is calling & I must go

I HAVE ISSUES

OF COURSE I TALK TO MYSELF
sometimes I need expert advice

Favorite Slogans on T-Shirts I've Folded

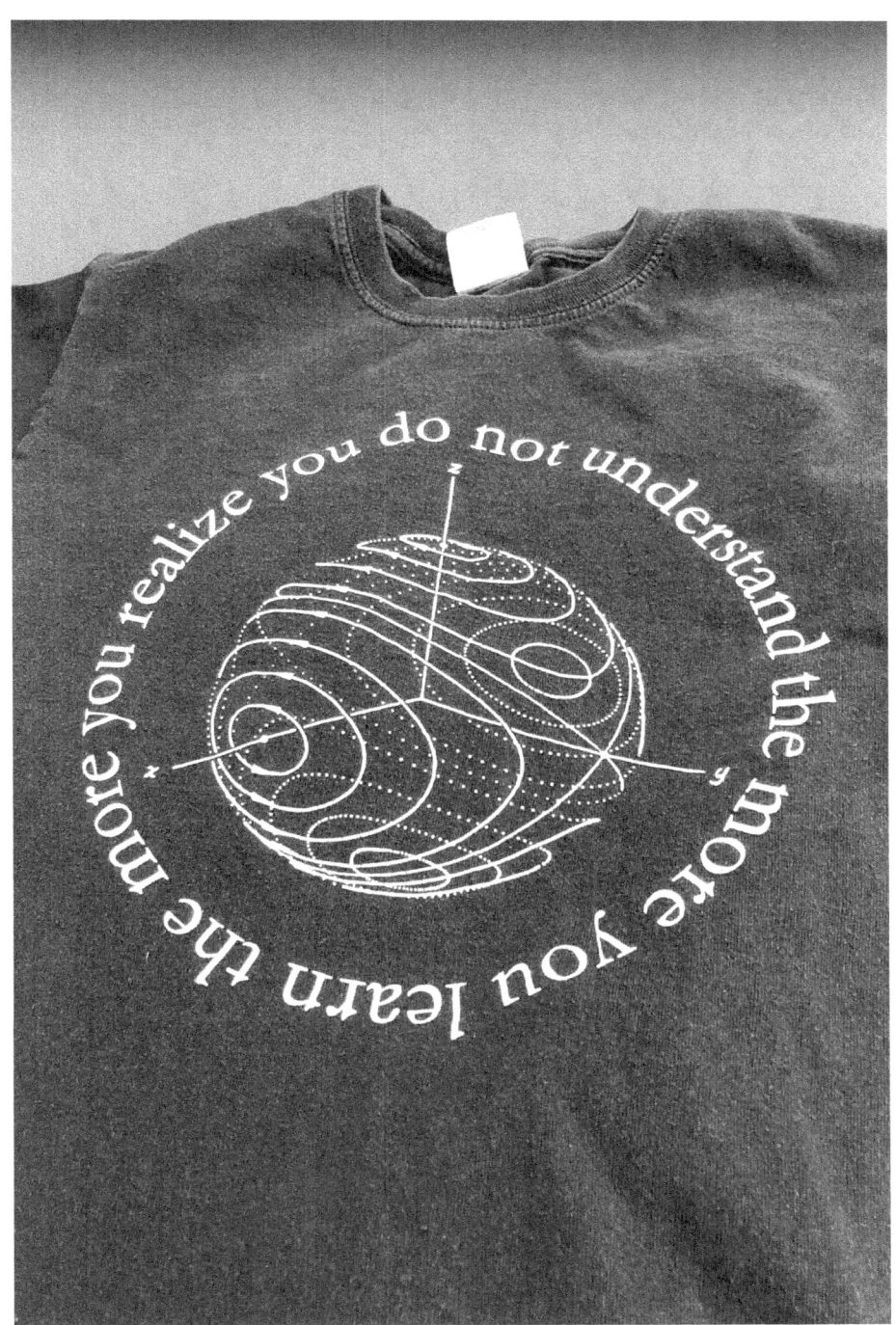

the more you realize you do not understand the more you learn

Doing Mr. Right's Laundry

Match.com and other online dating websites?
Too much weeding.
Speed Dating at lunch?
I usually just eat 2 meals a day.
Meetup app?
Scheduling nightmare, commuting time and COVID.
Recommendations from friends?
Everyone's partnered up and preoccupied.

I can see the benefits of a paid village matchmaker.

But at my age and temperament,
I'm not sure I really want to partner up.
If it's in the universe's master plan,
Mr. Right will have to drop down from the sky
right smack into my life.

Swiftly. Conveniently. Definitively.

Or in my world, drop down into our laundromat.
So, I remain on the lookout.
Like reading tea leaves or the lines in one's palm,
his drop off laundry will provide the necessary evidence
we are meant for each other.

For starters: no wheeled cart, trash bag or basic laundry basket.
Nope. My guy uses a sturdy nylon bag.
Sanitary. Private. Practical.

No hankies, for sure.
Definitely cotton knit boxers,
(accentuates the right bulges, more forgiving on others)
absolutely no briefs or baggy boxers.
A few t-shirts,
and not the thin white ones
but thicker, colored and

free of corporate or commercial logos
(he detests excessive American marketing too),
maybe a few from some old running or cycling races,
but nothing gaudy.
Surely a faded comfy sweatshirt,
with worn cuffs and a hood that lost a drawstring
a friend he can't pitch (he's known for his loyalty)
Jeans: Just 1 blue and 1 black pair (a fellow minimalist).
Straight legged: 34-34.
No Mom jeans: Levi's.
Bonus points: gray Carhartts.

What else will I find in my possibly true love's laundry?
Faded flannel pj bottoms.
A serviceable old towel or two.
Sheet set of cotton high thread count,
no microfiber or cold slippery nylon crap.

Possibly a curveball or two in his load requiring handwashing
which customers always slip in.
Perhaps a new red bandana
(serves as a napkin in his truck-camper or
a makeshift sling for an injured hiking partner).
Maybe a dog collar,
(I've always wanted a dog but never had time),
or a sheepskin lined wool cap with ear flaps
(he likes outdoor winter activities too).

And if the universe is being clear,
an omen:
an overlooked Milky Way wrapper
a library card in a pocket
a crumpled receipt from my favorite brew pub
a...

I'm waiting...
sort of.

The Art and Exercise of Mopping

The place is empty, so I sweep,
put out the yellow "Caution-wet floor" signs
and grace our hottest water with precious Lysol.
Stringed friend as a rudder,
I then steer the wheeled bucket toward the front door.

I'm ready for my mopping work out.
I operate my arms at a low height to preserve my rotatcr cuffs,
bend my legs so they can assist
and tighten those sleepy abs.

Who needs a gym membership?

I've perfected some moves:
the out and back pumping motion with one arm
(alternating sides is essential to promote symmetry)
the Figure 8
the windshield wiper
name-writing in cursive
and the classic two-handed side to side when boredom
    or fatigue set in.

I add extra elbow grease when needed
as I cover the 3,694 square feet I know so well.
The high traffic spots are engrained into my
mopping routine:
around the front rug
under the picnic tables
in front of the washers, changer, vending machine
and toilet, of course.

Goodbye:
soap drip spots
soda spills
sidewalk slop
smashed snacks
surprised spiders

and hopefully a few of my unwanted calories.

I Must Vent

Like our dryers with their
vertical
aluminum
tubes
sprouting
to the rooftop,

like our double run of
6-inch sewer lines with traps and drains,

like our HVAC system,

I, too, must vent.

The blowing off of excess
is necessary to prevent
overexpansion at least,
or dangerous explosions at worst.

I'm co-owner
but also clean,
wash, dry and fold orders.

So,
here I vent.

All customers:
Read our signs.
Don't make a mess in our bathroom.
Use the trash cans.
Don't leave your handprints all over the glass doors
    on the machines.
Be considerate. Share carts and folding tables.
Turn your cell phones off speaker or use headphones.

Don't complain about your piled up laundry when you come in.
Just do it more regularly.
You could donate or downsize your clothes and linens.
Hey, just simplify and go naked?

Drop off customers:
Turn your socks right-side out and your shirts and pants too.
Oh, and take your underwear off separately from your pants
    so they're not tangled up.
Plus check your pockets.
Tell me if you have brand new items hiding in your load
    that might bleed.
Why the heck do you have so much laundry for me
    to do anyway?
Have you considered going naked?

Dribblers:
For that food that didn't make it into your mouth and landed
    on your shirt covering your belly, diluted liquid dish soap
    works magic. Rub it in right away.
Wear a bib, use a napkin, slow down.
Use restraint since we Americans are over-consumers anyway.
Or maybe try eating naked?

People with lax potty habits:
Wipe your bum bums folks. You aren't four-years old anymore.

continued

We all have accidents but regular "Hershey highways"
  are unsanitary and signify laziness.
They are dirty, stinky and stain your underdrawers.
Who would ever want to sleep with you?
Wipe a few times. Moisten your TP. Use wet wipes.
  Get a bidet.
How about going naked and showering after each BM?

Pet owners:
Shake your pet bedding out before you even come in here.
Tell us after you've left a coating of pet hair in the washer
  so we can clean it out for the next person.
Vacuum your home regularly or pull up your dang carpeting
  or at least sweep with a frigin' broom.
Change your wardrobe to slick polyester so the
  pet hair doesn't cling.
Wear slippers or go barefoot so your socks aren't
  matted in hair.
How about a hairless breed instead?
If not, why don't you go naked like your pet?

Uh oh.
If everyone goes naked,
we'll be out of business.

[Deep breath and exhalation]
Venting is so therapeutic.
I feel much better now.

Staffing Woes

Worse than any stain,
like wine + blood + rust
with a little ground-in grease as well

more troublesome and time consuming
than fifty pairs of apron strings
twisted and unyielding in a Gordian knot

like Sisyphus,
damned to his eternal task
of pushing the boulder up the hill
only to have it roll back down each and every time

is our perpetual task of staffing.

Although I have read about robots that fold laundry
(expensive and limited capabilities, to date),
unless an owner has an unattended laundromat,
other humans are needed to help run it.

Hence the ongoing interviewing, hiring, firing,
training, managing, and placating of human staff.

If I could step back,
an outsider's view of this monstrous task would
be entertaining, even comical.

Candidates purport to really want the job
of a lowly laundromat attendant
but then fail to fully complete an application,
return phone calls for an interview or shadowing opportunity
or show-up at scheduled times.

continued

Some applications are unreadable, others overly detailed.
Many provide spouse, sibling or even their own
offspring as references.
Think 1:10 odds for weeding out a potential employee.

The creativity that candidates express during the
training and early employment phase is astounding.
Sick? Late? Not a good job fit?
Fabricate a reason:
the parent in the hospital
the dying grandmother (some seem to have 7)
the impromptu child school activity (even during a pandemic)
the lost dog
the faulty alarm clock

unreliable transportation contradicting assured reliability
   during interview
Why is it so difficult to be honest?

And for new and veteran employee scheduling glitches,
the cell phone is now the handy excuse.
It was misplaced, off, out of power, silenced,
borrowed by a spouse,
squirreled away by game-loving offspring.
Phone, guilty.
Phone owner, innocent.

And yes, we certainly live in texting times.
Our forefathers, or fore-employers,
could never have imagined getting a resignation letter
via text message minutes before a scheduled shift.

Every service industry has its own strategy for hiring:
Indeed
Facebook
Craigslist
Help Wanted sign
word of mouth
tips from blogs and industry specific journals.
It seems like it shouldn't be so difficult.

While we can offer some free laundry, tips and
an attendance bonus
we can't compete with Amazon, McDonalds and
big box stores.
Family-owned, fun, and flexible is hard to sell.

So, as I stretch out my arms
and lean into that boulder,
I envision the reliable, hardworking, happy, satisfied,
future employees that I know are out there,
just trying to find our laundromat.

Trough Filters and Their Kin

The nastiest chore on our checklist is
cleaning the trap in the trough drain.
It's a filter,
a piece of hard gray plastic the size of a cookie sheet
with pea sized perforations.

It rests vertically in the last trough,
attached in series, that all the washers'
wastewater dumps into under the covered bulkhead.
The filter catches muck and lets the
dirty water pass into the sewer pipe.

At least daily,
armed with rubber gloves,
the filter is removed from its resting spot
and slop scraped into the trash can with
a brush and paper towels.

Muck? Slop?
Blackish goo of hair, threads, dirt, plastic and paper bits,
stuffing from exploded pillows and other surprises.
Slimy and foul.

But a filter and regular cleaning
prevent a backed-up sewer line or a flood.
A grimy but vital chore.

As I scrub,
I'm reminded of other "filters":
lint drawers and screens in our dryers
little screens in our intake water lines
those ingenious color catching sheets which absorb
excessive dyes in a mixed wash load.

continued

59

At home, other kin:
my favorite of all filters, the white pleated paper circle
pressed in a plastic cone
which catches grounds and lets the precious coffee drip
down into my waiting mug.
The multitude of others residing in the kitchen:
colanders of all sizes and perforations,
metal or mesh scooped-shaped strainers with handles,
tea balls and even tea bags,
simple citrus juicers
shaker tops and grinders for salt and pepper and other herbs
cheesecloth.
Do dish drainers count?

More unassuming filters dwell in the home:
window screens, vent filter in the oven hood
plus the furnace filter
also any faucet and hose screens
certainly floor drains with punched hole covers
and in sinks, tubs and shower drains, too.

In cars, there are oil filters, cabin air filters, others too I bet.

My firewall on my computer, a comb,
face masks in this COVID era…
Dare I go on?

No need,
this nasty chore is completed.
I slide the trap back down into its slot where it stands
unobstructed,
ready and waiting
for tomorrow's slop.

I ~~Try Not to~~ Judge

Honestly, as I wash dry and fold
your laundry order here in our laundromat
I will not judge you for your:

~~teeny tiny~~ thong underwear ~~that looks painful to wear~~
~~pathetic padded push-up~~ bras
~~rag bag quality~~ undershirts
pajama sets ~~that are holey, stretched out and coffee~~
  ~~or wine stained~~
~~your choice of~~ boxers vs. briefs
~~overtaxed~~ spanks
~~strategically ripped~~ jeans
blouses ~~with "cold shoulders" or other peek-a-boo holes~~
tank tops ~~with spray tan stains~~
t-shirts ~~with slogans of poor taste~~
~~weekly food stains on the fronts of all the~~ shirts
~~smoke-scented~~ load
~~lifeless~~ sweaters ~~ready for Goodwill~~
uniforms ~~with tacky company logos~~
~~threadbare~~ bedding
pillowcases ~~covered with make-up stains~~
~~pet hair smothered~~ clothing and linens
socks ~~with the bottoms embedded with all kinds of floor crap~~
laundry basket ~~so old, brittle and cracked it might cut my hands~~

I do try, mostly.

But then you pick up your order and
are genuinely grateful I did your laundry and
poof
those judgements disintegrate.

Chapter 3

Customers with Impact

Essential to any business are customers.
At our mat, we have drop-off as well as pick-up
and delivery customers who pay per pound for us
to do their laundry. But most customers come in,
and use the machines themselves. Many of these
do-it-yourself (DIY) customers turn into regulars.
Some leave lasting impressions.

Our Secret

Beige t-shirts and slacks,
beige socks and
beige bath towels
in a striped beige canvas basket
comprise the bulk of your
weekly drop-off laundry.

Despite some muted gray undies
and an occasional navy or olive garment,
"vanilla"
is how the other attendants
described you from your laundry.
Colorless, drab, boring.

Irrelevant to me.
You're a polite and patient regular,
pleasant to chat with
and a faithful tipper.

Middle-aged with
medium build
perhaps a
cartographer,
geologist,
writer?

continued

Then one day,
a coal black fleece jacket
appears in your laundry.
It has padded shoulders,
hidden zipped pockets,
flaps of extra fabric
and a strip of Velcro atop the hood
to attach some mysterious object.

It awaits your chain mail and metal helmet as
you, a knight,
joust and perform other gallant acts at Renaissance Fairs.

It protects your arms and
stabilizes your plastic helmet with headlamp as
you, a spelunker,
descend ropes into yawning caverns and
slither through treacherous tight spots.

It safely stows precious samples in pockets
and secures a recording camera on your hood as
you, a fossil hunter,
seek that dinosaur across remote rocky ruins.

Vanilla? Definitely not.

No worries.
Your secret is safe with me.

Cathy, the Cat Lady

You load the machines with pillows,
blankets, stuffed toys and cat beds
from the 15+ rescues you nurture.
Then you sit by our front window,
basking in the sun looking out.

Occasionally you read a magazine
but never watch TV or play on your cell phone.

If you have a takeout meal,
you eat it with full attention.

Sometimes you exchange pleasantries with other customers,
but mostly you just observe and keep to yourself.

A few times,
you startle me amid a cleaning chore,
and are suddenly sociable.

You seek my companionship to discuss
your health
your busy day
your heavy workload for your age
the weather or current event
or a mundane magazine morsel.

You never ask how I'm doing.

I clean up the cat litter, hair and foam
from exploded pet beds left in your wake
as I watch you pack up and drive off
but I'm not fooled.

Even though you haven't coughed up a hairball, yet,
I know you are truly a feline in human flesh.

Big Jim

You unfolded your 6ft 4 frame from your ancient blue Corolla
and lumbered in on swollen bowed legs with
a small white trash bag of laundry in each hand.
Before you disappeared, you came weekly.

You always used bigger machines than needed,
heavy on the soap and bleach plus a wash cycle upgrade.
You carefully folded and placed your dried items
in fresh bags to carry back to your car.
You explained your mama taught you the importance
of cleanliness
Though you disappeared, I'd vouch you honored her legacy.

While your clothes washed, you requested I sit and talk.
A break for your loneliness and my fatigue.
We'd share stories about family, working and health challenges.
I overlooked that you're a talker.
You overlooked that I'm distracted.
When you disappeared, you were only 15 years ahead of me.

Sometimes you surprised me with coffee, a donut or
chicken pot pie from the grocery store next door.
You rarely let me reciprocate, claiming you
only wanted water to take your medicine with.
Until you disappeared, I equated your presence with kindness.

You were one of our earliest and most faithful customers.
You told friends and strangers about our laundromat.
You gave us business advice and basic encouragement.
Despite that you disappeared, you were our #1 fan.

When you met my father on his inaugural tour of the place
you two discussed politics (surprisingly both Trump supporters!),
changing times and traveling through Louisiana.
Two old men, one black the other white,
trading stories over a laundromat picnic table.
You gave me a heartfelt card when my own dear mama passed.
Athough you disappeared, you made strong connections here.

You dropped off little gifts.
We took you out for Italian food.
Then, a long gap of
countless unanswered phone messages.
I didn't even know your last name, address, next of kin.
Finally, you picked up, voice weak as a kitten.
Illness, sudden hospitalization and rehab I learned.
Didn't even have a bag packed you confessed.
Help now lined up at home and a promise
to return to the mat when stronger but first,
three months of mail demanded attention.
Next, the pandemic, a declining parent and
struggling business depleted my energy.
Months later I phoned again
but got a woman's voice,
number reassigned.

Early on in our budding friendship
you confided that you were not good with goodbyes
and would just disappear at some point.
To Louisiana where niece and old property reside
or to finally be with your mama.

To this day
when an old blue Toyota parks in front of the mat,
my heart lifts.
Hope surpasses logic.

Roger, an Irregular Regular

You greet me with "Hey Lady"
since you can never remember my name.
You blare out:
"I'm setting my stuff here."
"I'm going to buy donuts next store."
"I'm heading to use the bathroom."
"The bus is here."
"I'll be back again on Thursday."
loud enough for the full laundromat to hear.

You still explain about your shaking hands
but I don't mind at all to help you:
put coins from the changer into your pill bottle where you
    store them
feed quarters into washers or dryers
pick up a runaway coin you dropped
smooth out and insert dollar bills into your wallet
retrieve a can of soda from the vending machine
stuff your laundry in the bag wedged between the handles
    of your walker
or even fold it, including your wife's underwear (new, you tell
    me) when you're rushed.

I'm not surprised by the questions you ask other customers or
what information you share with them including your
age, along with your wife's
social security check amount, and her's too
trailer rent
bills
holiday BBQ menu
medical appointment details.

And it doesn't bother me, in fact I relish your:
outdoor voice always used inside
unabashed belches
sticky spots and crumbs left behind
"Darn it anyways."

You are one of the many teachers in my life.
You've revealed how decades of
conditioning, brainwashing and insecurities
have added layers of insulation over my authentic self,
the child I once was.

And I'm trying to undo them.

Alice and the Tribe

You do 3 to 4 bags of laundry
every week or two.

So that's a lot of laundry
added up over the years
especially as you just turned 90.

Since we chat during your visits here, I know you've had
3 husbands,
several kids,
dozens of grandkids and great grandkids.

I also know you live in a double wide
on the remnant of the old farm
now sold and whittled away
with a street named after your husband's family.

And believe it or not,
I know you worked in a laundromat years ago
so I jokingly try to hire you
and you longingly wish to accept
and relive that time or
perhaps get respite from your current life.
Which, I don't know.

But I know for certain
you are a member of the tribe of special women.
Women with hunched backs and gnarled fingers
and short no-nonsense hairstyles.
Women whose flexed posture and
worn, crooked joints were shaped by bending over:
serving husbands
cooing fussy babies on their lap
stirring a pot on the stove
quilting or crocheting or sewing

continued

writing a treasured recipe to share
picking up sticks in the yard
wrestling a stubborn gate for a waiting tractor
coaxing vegetables from the earth
reading a bible or fingering a rosary.

I know other members of this tribe.

My mom was one,
and many of my hearty aunts of the Midwest,
some older ladies from the church
and definitely other women who have
graced this laundromat
toting or pushing or wheeling the
dirty laundry they'll tend.

Women, who let's say,
did not have a good life,
or more accurately, an easy one.

Women who gave their bodies and energy and time
to family,
community,
God.

Alice,
may you and the tribe
know my respect and gratitude.
May you all find peace someday
if not in this life,
then the next.
Perhaps in some new shape and form,
one that is pain-free and glistening and
moves about with ease and delight,
and that angels, unicorns and fairies
are serving you.

Our Precious Perceiving Eyes

I saw you and after a few visits, figured it out.

It was not your:
slower, wide-based gait
tall, thin, hunched posture
pale skin
dyed hair
nicked up shins or
disheveled appearance that gave it away.

No, it was that you:
held your cell phone 2 inches from your eyes
tried to put your laundry in washers already taken
had trouble figuring out the machine buttons
spent 15 minutes in the bathroom
took forever to dry and fold your laundry
and left a trail of forgotten items in your wake.

You are a middle-aged man navigating the world
with reduced vision,
a symptom of albinism.

But over time,
you've gotten familiar with this place.

Sometimes you come in without laundry for our free WiFi.
Please use.
I overhear you on your phone
talking with insurance agents, health care professionals,
customer care folks.
I send you a prayer of fortitude.
Or you come in just to eat a snack at our picnic table
or to study the coupon flyers.
You are welcome to linger.
Once you sorted financial papers in our well-lit front area.
Good luck.

continued

A few times,
I've driven by you at night walking on the darkened
sidewalks nearby
swinging our free laundry bag in your hand.
Contents:
groceries?
QuikTrip snacks or supplies?
borrowed linens?
clothes to stay with friends?
I hope you have ample friends.

Anyway,
be careful out there.
I hope we see each other again soon.

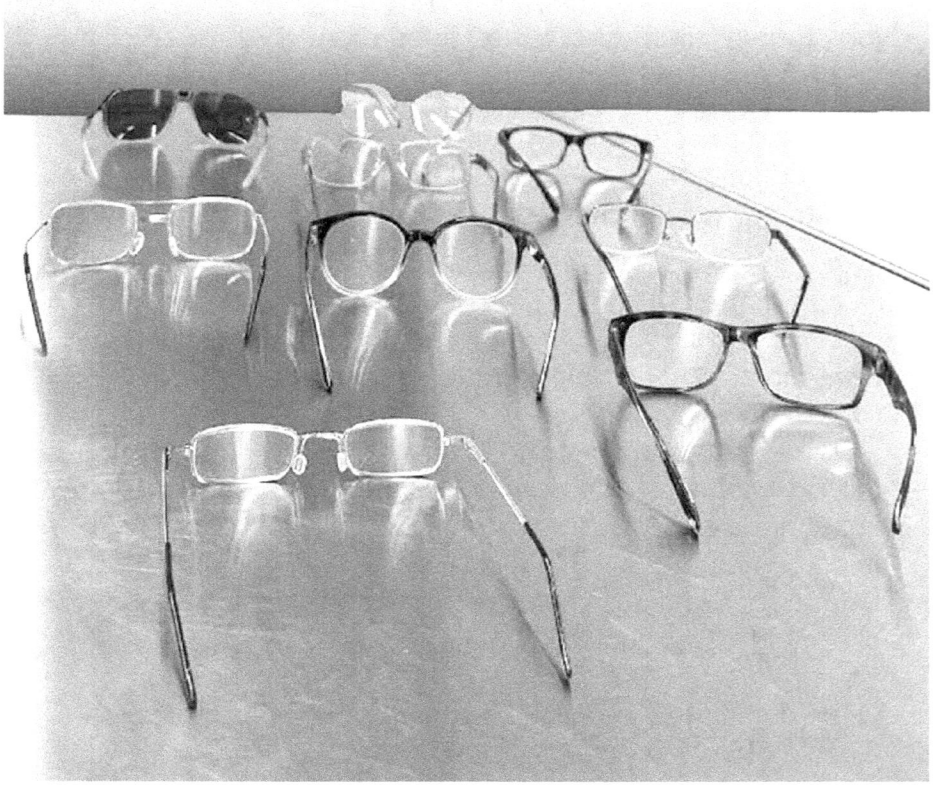

Julia, The Enlightened

I learn your name later.
It's an abbreviated form of a unique longer name, Verjulia.
You are elegant, calm and articulate.
Julia, a black queen.

We first meet when an angry customer
is rude to me. I am crushed.
You see my pain.
"You don't know what that person is facing today.
Let it go."
Julia, the psychologist.

I watch you patiently instruct your
lovely teenage daughters on the skill of laundry.
Side by side you show and explain how to
sort, load, gauge soap and operate the machines.
Julia, the teacher.

You describe how you are guiding your eldest to be a
financially responsible adult.
Your system includes a checking account,
her deposited paychecks,
and regular portions paid to you for her
cell phone and living expenses while under your roof.
Your sole goal is her eventual
foolproof independence.
Julia, the pragmatic parent.

Over your visits you share your journey to lose some weight,
get more fit, eat healthier.
We chat about lifting weights, recipes, thrift store shopping.
Julia, fellow pilgrim.

continued

You always request to watch HGTV between loads.
You and your husband are saving for a modest house.
Relaxed and detached, you absorb the information.
No comments, sighs or shrieks.
You know the proper value of things and
aren't swayed by pageantry and pretension.
Julia, the objective consumer.

When I ask how your day is going
sometimes you recite scripture.
You convey its relevance and impact.
You minister through words and actions.
Julia, the Preacher.

You confide you are disheartened when a volunteer
mission trip abroad is cancelled due to COVID-19,
but explain it has taught you about selfishness
and expectations.
You find a self-improvement lesson in disappointment.
Julia, the Buddha.

On the spectrum of evolved human beings
You are far, far to the right, dear Julia.

You have graced our laundromat with
your insight, your presence, your example.

Power to the Snappers

There is a subpopulation of customers
that I honor in our laundromat.
Snappers
are kin to vintners, cheesemakers,
fine carpenters,
novelists and others who instill time and skill into
a chosen craft.

No heaving balled-up wet laundry from the cart
into the dryer.
Never.
This special society knows better.

Some novices or half-hearted Snappers
pull pieces apart from the mass of wet clothes,
fluff and toss into the dryer.
More like a carefree wave of the hand,
nevertheless, loosening does occur.

continued

Other Snappers grab handfuls and
employ a quick flick or two sideways
to flap open the clothing
before the forceful lateral fling into the dryer.
Reminiscent of the bicycle riding boy's
newspaper delivery onto a front lawn.

Veteran Snappers
tease apart the twisted orb
pluck out individual elements and double-handedly
snap it
sharply up and down.
A space alien might think this
Snapper is paying homage to a shiny heating machine.

Maybe Snapping should be
taught in high school home economics class,
trained during marriage preparation and
included in mandatory screening of all political candidates.

The benefit of snapping?
Shorter drying time and
in my opinion, less wrinkles.

So that upfront investment in time and energy
reveals patience and foresight
which results in a better outcome.

Onward Snappers!
The world needs you.

My Prayer
for the Kids Who Wear this Laundry

I don't mind scraping dried macaroni off onesies or
dumping out crumbs buried in fuzzy slippers.
And I always check the bounce in the netting of a tutu
or Frozen Princess dress as I take it off the drying rack.
While folding silly Christmas pjs, I pretend
my fond reminiscing will multiply their holiday magic.
I hang the mini polo shirts and school uniforms with care
just like their older counterparts.
With my hands I smooth out and neatly stack
training underwear covered in Marvel characters.
Even the poop I discover in kids' dirty underwear
is more tolerable, honestly, than adults'.

And I say a prayer for these kids
who will wear this laundry I wash.

May their imagination be unlimited as they play with abandon
Princess Elsa or Spiderman or Luke Skywalker.
Work shall come.

And I wish that at least a few
of their holiday wishes come true,
so they taste the end result of hope.
Cynicism and sadness loom.

And I pray that someday, a spark of gratitude erupts
for clean clothes or the macaroni on the spoon
or bodily functions that work,
for bed and a good night's sleep.
A future day of providing for self and others shall dawn.

continued

Certainly, I desire the basics for them, for all kids,
safety, sustenance, curiosity, knowledge, opportunity.
Violence, intolerance, disinformation lurk nearby.

And since I've witnessed and experienced the
erosive power of stress and anxiety,
I implore any and all heavenly forces
to keep the grappling hands of fear far, far away.

But mostly
for these unspoiled ones
I pray they experience some pure joy,
in their own fashion,
in these clean little clothes,
during this brief time in their lives.
For that joy will spawn the desire for more joy.
And joy shall carry them forward.

Chapter 4

How to Handle a Talker
Series

Working in a laundromat allows you to scrutinize and talk with people. Because DIY customers are there for an hour or so, that chunk of time allows for conversations and confidences to develop. Like to their barber, bartender, minister or masseuse, customers often engage you, the lowly laundromat attendant. Over time, I've developed different strategies on how to identify and interact with different types of talkers.

How to Handle a Talker: The Gusher

There is no stopping you.

Like the water gushing into the washer
after the green start button is pushed,
you gush forth at me in our mat.

Urgently. Uncontrollably. Unapologetically.

The gushing is confined to some single currently
all-consuming topic like the:
broken old washing machine
broken new washing machine
first face to face date tonight since the pandemic started
incompetent service technician
latest political upheaval
unavailable part due to supply chain disruptions
crappy laundry facility at your rental
countless reasons why you're the busiest person in the world
flooded basement
great new job you started resulting in laundry pile up
lazy kids
daughter's wedding
shocking new medical diagnosis.

Sensing the onslaught, I
rearrange my stance into acceptance,
soften my face to portray interest and
remind myself of the pointlessness of any dialogue.

Most gushes are powerful but short.

After your outburst
you seem refreshed,
like the emerging laundry released of dirt.

I, too, am relieved,
and amazed at how my inaction has helped you,
a gusher.

How to Handle a Talker: The Dripper

You start a conversation upon sighting me,
even before you get your laundry into a machine.

If I disappear briefly from your orbit
you pick up where you left off and
segue into numerous and sundry topics:
the when, why and how you do your laundry
details about the laundry products you are using
your pet's condition or amazing antics
your breakfast, lunch and supper menu
your purchases next door at the grocery store
your health
your detailed schedule after finishing your laundry.

You are like a slow steady drip,
unrelenting and wasteful.

There is no true conversation between us.
Like a faucet missing a rubber washer,
you are unable to control
the constant dribble of words.

With you,
I must avoid asking any questions,
as they only enhance the flow.
Declarative statements like
"Glad to see you!"
"You're looking good today!"
"Looks like it's laundry day!"
merely shift but
do not dampen the flow.

Ideally, I must avoid eye contact or proximity
(suddenly office paperwork beckons!)
Otherwise, I must just
tune out the irritating drip
as I try to be productive in your presence
since a leak can be a headache to fix.

How to Handle a Talker: The Expert

I do not waste my breath
when you confront me.

You were or are
an engineer
a technician
handy, in your opinion.

You have
worked on laundry equipment
gone to many laundromats
done tons laundry in your lifetime
talked to other customers who concur with you,
the laundromat expert.

According to the expert
our front loaders:
don't have enough water
don't make enough bubbles
don't do a good job
cost too much
have confusing buttons or soap dispensers
and our dryers aren't hot enough
don't hold enough
and are overpriced too.

The expert has reasons, case stories,
hunches, explanations and solutions.

Just like when I
try to decipher a mystifying product manual
am perpetually "on hold" with customer support or
sit poised for a response during an e-chat for tech help
the expert, also makes me feel powerless.

I know it's futile to fume or be rude.

Rather, I
lower my expectation for any positive outcome
envision a future scenario of happy customers and
working machines
and know this interaction will pass since
the expert shall eventually move on and
bestow his or her expertise elsewhere.

How to Handle a Talker: The Joyful

You've been in a few times,
so are comfortable with the space, staff, machines.

If you talk on the phone
it's always brief.
You chat freely and warmly
with me and other customers.

You exude gratitude as you divulge about your:
upcoming day surgery (postponed twice by COVID)
time off to prepare
ability to quickly do your laundry in our big machines
aunt who told you about our mat
elderly mom who is still alive
kids who irritate you but help you
life despite its challenges.

You smile,
hum,
sing,
and when
you laugh,
it's not a chuckle, guffaw or hee-hee.
It is an authentic, deep and rich bellow
coming from your solar plexus.

I sweep the floor around you endlessly and
the machines in your area have never been shinier.
I:
hover
watch
listen
but mostly absorb.
Like a color catching sheet we throw in mixed loads to
absorb excess dye in the washer,
I just want to take in more of your essence.

How to Handle a Talker: The Bester

Like the ads in slick laundry trade magazines
urging purchase of the latest, greatest, most
revolutionary washer,
you aim to best every talking point in our chat.

Though we are acquaintances born from this laundry space
despite our nearly nonexistent shared history
you are compelled to outdo me.

You engage me in conversation,
steer it toward the topic of your choosing
then proceed to dominate regarding:
an amazing trip you took vs. my humdrum one
the impact of cancelling your next amazing trip
    vs. my nonexistent one
your telephone customer service nightmare
    vs. my simple irritation
your horrible car repair saga vs. my mere clipped
    driver's mirror
the insurmountable quagmire within your family
    vs. my simple friction
your latest health challenge vs. mine, a pimple in comparison.

A segue to a new topic is fruitless
as you are an Olympian Bester in all realms of life.

I know I can never win with you
or even tie
for your eyes are only on the trophy.

When I encounter you, these are the keys:
recognize the game as it is starting
don't pick up the ball, club, or sword
award praise quickly, if mandatory,
then swiftly exit the stadium.

Who wants to always be the best anyway?

How to Handle a Talker: The Self

It's a pleasure to have your company here,
since we enjoy our time together
and the conversation never drags.
You know all my favorite topics
plus, we share the same political views.
I'm convinced I can confide all my skeletons
but it seems you already know about them.

I savor our talks:
mindless chatter
reworked verbal arguments
stimulating ideas
problem solving strategies
teeth-gnashing regrets
schemes and dreams for the future.

Amid our exchange
I look up from my task
and the one-way mirror by our back office
reveals in astonishing clarity
that the you I've been talking with
is me.

No wonder I so readily have your ear.

Upon this discovery I
laugh
try not to berate
realize that the self is like the other that I
need to listen and respond to with care.

So then,
I continue talking.

Chapter 5

Detritus

Detritus (noun) per Merriam Webster Dictionary
1. geology: loose material (such as rock fragments or organic particles) that results directly from disintegration
2. a. a product of disintegration, destruction, or wearing away: debris
    b. miscellaneous remnants: odds and ends

When we clean the machines, we find detritus. These are things caught in washers, dryer drums and lint drawers. Some small items get swept down through the washer lines into the trough or trapped in the filter. Odds and ends are also dropped on the floor when loading up laundry or simply left behind on the tops of machines or folding tables. Over the last few years, we tossed the detritus into a plastic bin. The following list is just a subset of this treasure trove which spawned some fictional backstories and creative photos.

Washer and Dryer Detritus

candy wrappers
wadded paper, mostly receipts
lots of coins
very clean $1 bills
Chapstick
tiny Lego pieces
pens
a tablet stylus (repeatedly returned to the customer)
guitar picks
foam ear plugs
fake fingernails
liberated underwires from bras
escaped pads from swimsuits or sports bras
ejected plastic collar stays from men's dress shirts
buttons, safety pins
miscellaneous garters, elastic straps, odd buckles
strange plastic objects
lighters
vape devices
nails, screws, bolts and nuts
little Allen wrenches
utility knife razor blades
bullets and empty casings
batteries
Band-Aids
paper clips and binder clips
keys, always single
gift cards, usually for pizza
plastic key cards for hotel rooms
elastic hair bands, bobby pins, barrettes
cheap, thin, black plastic combs
religious medals and pendants for necklaces
rings and earrings
a tooth

The Liberated Bra Underwire

It was born of sheet metal
flattened, curved and tips rounded
by a machine in China
then shoved into a tight white fabric tunnel
by human hands
in the allotted 2.3 seconds per garment.

A glued-on rose separated it from its twin.

Four other pairs of hands along a
bustling assembly line completed the creation:
a 38C white, lacey, but practical bra.
Packaged with 47 other clones it left the factory.

Though cushioned by somewhat stiff poly-cotton fabric the
wire bounced and jerked within the box on its first truck ride.
Next came the slow peaceful boat trip
to a new land in a cargo container
followed by a brief gentle sway from a massive crane.
More trucking was punctuated by hibernations in warehouses
until arriving at a Walmart.

Bigger American hands, one pair,
plucked the bra from its packaging,
stuck it on a hanger and then a hook.

Suspended, it remained there for 8 days
despite 3 customers trying it on.
One lady returned and
tossed the item into a loaded cart,
scanned, bagged and brought it home.

Gradually, the underwire molded
to the shape of the owner,
albeit causing some abrasions at first.
It withstood forces and strain from the wearer
bending, stooping, briskly walking and
occasionally lifting other humans,

continued

some young and small, others old and frail.
Plus at least twice daily,
a car shoulder strap pressed the wire against a chest.

The underwire rested when the bra dangled from a doorknob
at the end of the day.
And after a few days the owner tossed it into a hamper.

She washed it in cold water on a delicate cycle and
let it air dry at the local laundromat.
But once a young boy tossed it in the washer
with t-shirts on hot and it shrunk.

The fabric tunnel got snugger.

More bending, reaching, hugging and compressing ensued.
Then the rose sheared off and
some stitches at the end of the tunnel (on the
right side) popped.

Once the owner noticed the underwire protruding
she forced it back in,
planned to mend it, but forgot.

Overlooked in the hamper,
the bra was hauled to the laundromat.

The 1,200 rpm of the washer was the final straw.
The underwire, extruded from its tunnel,
got caught in the washer drum holes.

The wet laundry was removed
but the wire stayed wedged in.
Later, the attendant noticed it while cleaning the machine,
extracted it with pliers
then tossed the liberated underwire into a plastic bin
with other washer and dryer detritus,
it's final resting spot,
far, far from its birthplace.

The Band-Aid

Could she blame it on:
the NFL?
Superbowl Sunday?
her boyfriend for requesting her famous homemade guacamole?
her aunt who first introduced her to the yummy dip?
the grocery store for having unripe produce?
Mexico for growing avocados?
the weird fruit itself with its thick pimpled skin?

She had to be honest.
It was her own rushing.

Instead of holding the dark green oval against the cutting board
with the widespread fingers of her left hand and
making that first careful shallow incision to guide the
following longer lengthwise cut
in haste,
she had vigorously hacked at it.
But the darn thing bounced and
rolled on the board in retaliation
and the knife continued downward
slashing the next available target
her left index finger.
Just past the last knuckle
into the pad of the tip,
the flesh accepted,
then stopped, the knife.

She refused a trip to the ER
but there was a lot of blood,
the paper towels in the kitchen trashcan as evidence.
And the first three Band-Aids got so bloody they wouldn't stick.

continued

She talked her boyfriend through the recipe.
They still had the party,
but she didn't drink much and
kept an ice pack on her hand.

One week later
she marvels at the healing scar,
a thin pink line,
a skin bridge,
a surprise
now revealed.

At the laundromat leaning against the folding table
facing a row of front load washers
she wonders if the fragile bridge will hold.

The morning's Band-Aid gone
but not missing.

She knows exactly where it is.
Sloshing with her clothes in the washer straight ahead.

The Ejected Collar Stay

Just under 2 inches
white
smooth flexible plastic
rounded point on one end

mini popsicle stick?
make up applicator?
bookmark?

A confused customer examined the object
after extracting it from under the dryer baffle
where it was pinned.
Unidentified,
she discarded it on the folding table.

Earlier at the same table
a young man plopped down a huge laundry basket
overflowing with laundry, hangers and soap jugs.
Masked,
he quickly stuffed all his laundry into one four-load washer.
He used to separate loads like his mom taught him,
nice shirts on permanent press, whites in hot, darks in cold.
Why, anymore?
After strolling to the store next door
he returned to eat the snack in his car rather than inside.
I'm so sick of the words "social distancing."
Once it dried,
he unloaded the tangled mess of laundry into a wheeled cart.
Amidst the towels, sweatpants, t-shirts and bed linens were
two wrinkled dress shirts.
Not too bad. Plaids camoflouge a lot.
As he grabbed his plastic hangers,
he remembered his pre-pandemic norm of
hanging eight shirts on his weekly laundromat visit.

continued

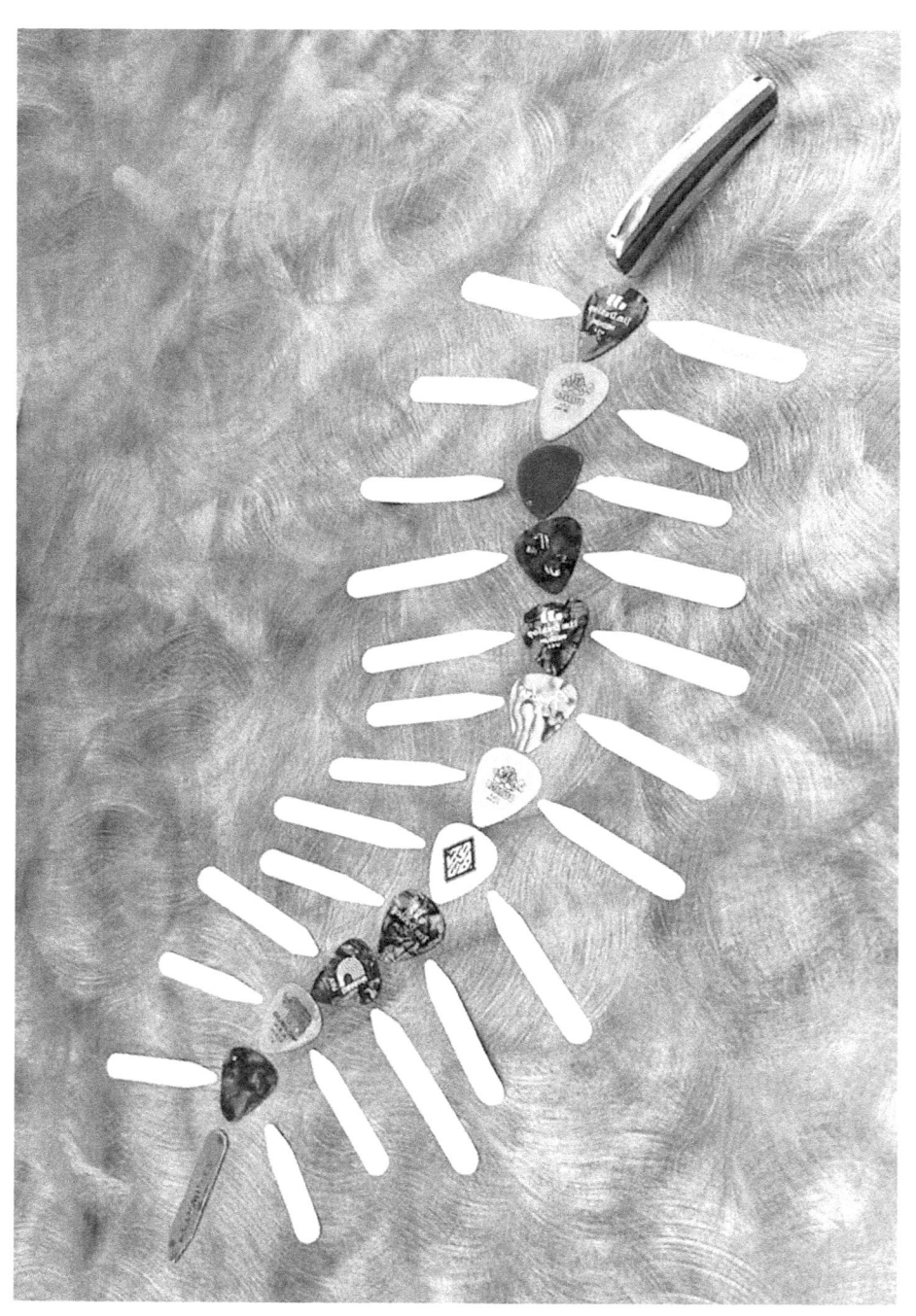

Centipede
Collar stays, guitar picks, pocket knife

One for each workday, one for church and two backups.
Now, in this working from home era with Zoom meetings
one shirt a week was enough.
I still like a spare.
Just as he spotted an open folding table, he stopped.
I'd rather go home and watch something on Netflix.
So, he crammed everything unfolded back in the basket
and draped the shirts on top.

The next workday,
a last-minute Zoom meeting was called.
He jumped up,
whipped off his t-shirt,
darted to his bedroom,
grabbed a plaid shirt on top of the clean laundry mountain
and bolted back to his home office area orbiting the sofa.

As he clicked "Join meeting"
he was still buttoning.
As colleagues faces and upper torsos blinked on
he realized his collar felt funny,
kind of limp on one side.
As his own face in a cube appeared on screen,
he realized the predicament.
The shirt looked a little off, asymmetrical.
Too late to change shirts.
Should I just push the laptop further back on the coffee table?
Instead
he faked a coughing attack,
hit "Mute" and "Stop Video"
and slipped out the remaining collar stay
before returning to the meeting,
now,
totally balanced.

The Fake Fingernail

Her first time
a splurge
all her friends had them
$29.99 special
N&G's Nails,
the convenient salon at Walmart in front of all the registers,
acrylic
plum raisin passion
with a single tiny rhinestone embedded on each index fingernail.

Immediately,
while swiping her credit card to pay for them,
she adored the shiny oval spears
more the color of cabernet than plums or raisins.

Her admiration of them continued
using her cell phone while driving,
and putting on makeup in the mirror each morning.
She also appreciated the high-pitched clicks on the
computer keyboard, new and mesmerizing sounds.
However,
she had to adjust how she used her fingers
to press buttons,
open drawers,
and feel small items with her finger pads
without the interference of sturdy overhanging nails.

A week later,
she felt some strain while pulling
the clothes out of the dryer at the laundromat
but disregarded it while talking on the
cell phone pinned between her shoulder and ear.

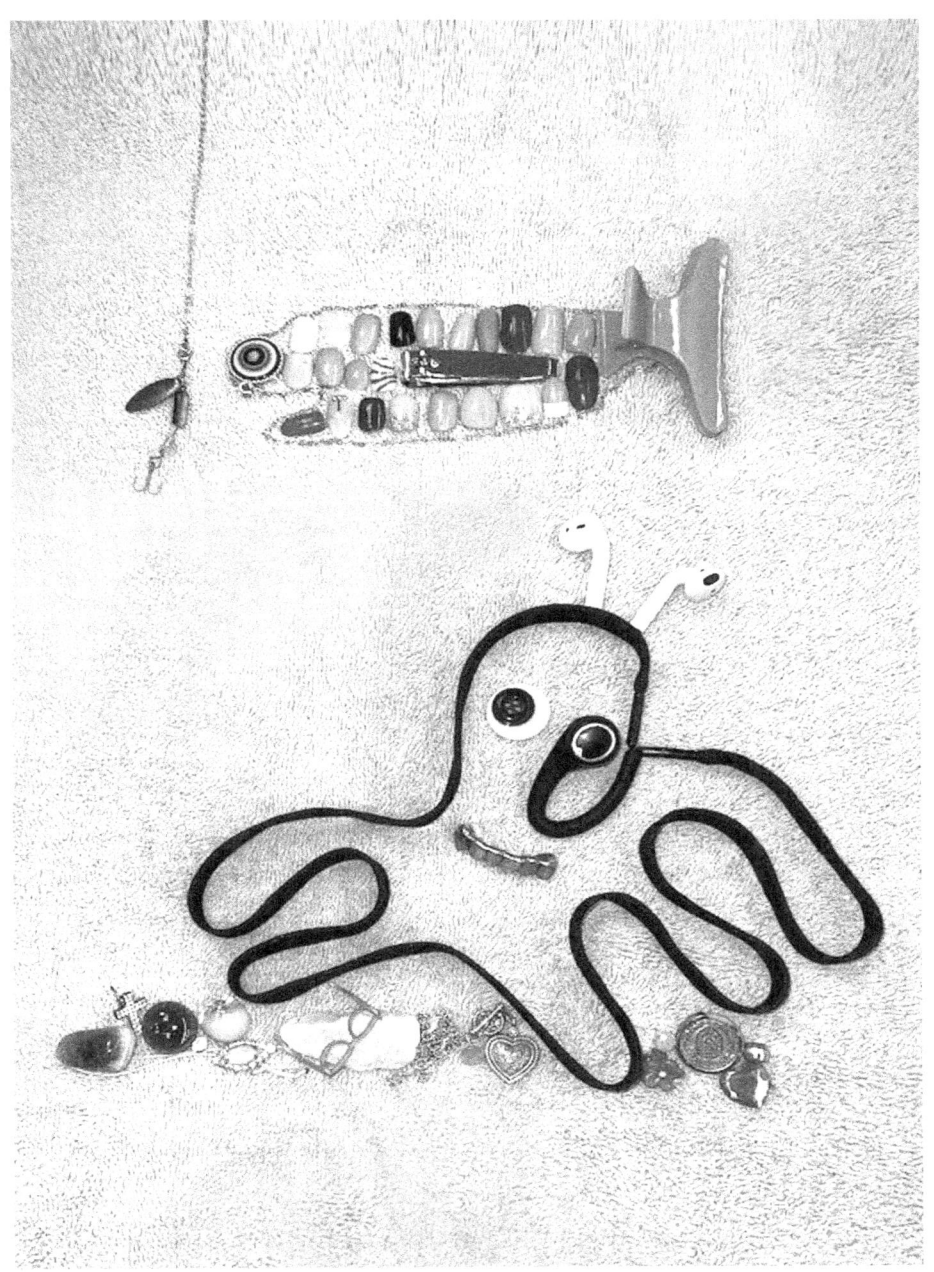

Sea Creatures

Fake fingernails, jewelry, ear buds, nail clipper, shoelace, fish hook

continued

Preoccupied and rushed to catch her TV show,
she stuffed the laundry into the
tall white basket and raced home.
She didn't notice her naked nail until
folding clothes while watching her show from the sofa.

She was minus one fake nail.
It made her God-given fingernail seem shabby and inept.
For a minute she looked around thinking she might be lucky
to spot it on her lap,
in the basket,
on the floor,
like a fallen leaf,
flower petal
or Post-it note.

Then she remembered the tug while
wrestling the clothes out of the dryer.

She could visualize the curved jewel
caught in the corner of the huge gray drum of dryer #27,
or perhaps by now,
tumbling with the next customers' wet clothes.

She wondered (since she was new at this)
how much does a single nail cost?

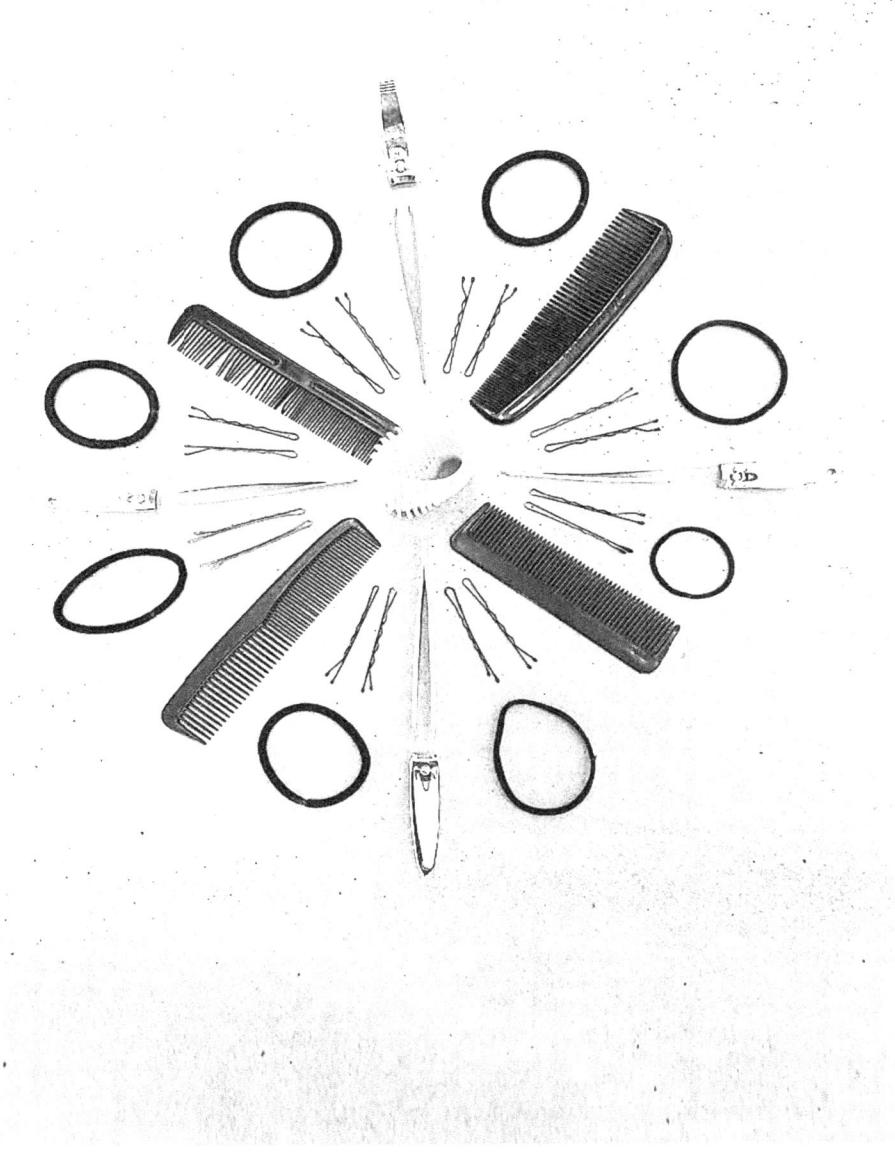

Star of the Mat

Combs, nail clippers, tweezers, bobby pins, hair bands & a curler

The Tooth

The second round had 42
replacing the 28
smaller, sharper versions.

They did their job.
Hard food
soft food
bones
sticks
some tasty slippers
the occasional nips at unruly children
and only once,
a solid bite in the fleshly calf of a teenager
from down the street who hopped the fence
to steal a seemingly unattended soccer ball.

Maybe it was the table scraps
or age
or gum disease.
(How many pet owners brush their pet's
teeth like the vet recommends?)

But in the end,
it was the sock chew toy
for the undoing.

In the daily wrestling match with
the brown-eyed boy
whose sudden yank
against the sideways jerk of a furry head
caused the unstable left top incisor
to be released from its soft pink home
of more than ten human years.

And then there were 41 remaining.

The freed tooth lodged in the sock toy
which also absorbed a surprisingly
scant amount of blood.
Three weeks later
the large round pet bed,
two blankets and the sock toy
were carted to the laundromat
and washed.

Later that day,
something hard clanged against
the washer drum wall as the attendant
sanitized the machine using a cloth rag.
Not the expected coin or button or screw

but a jagged oral pearl.

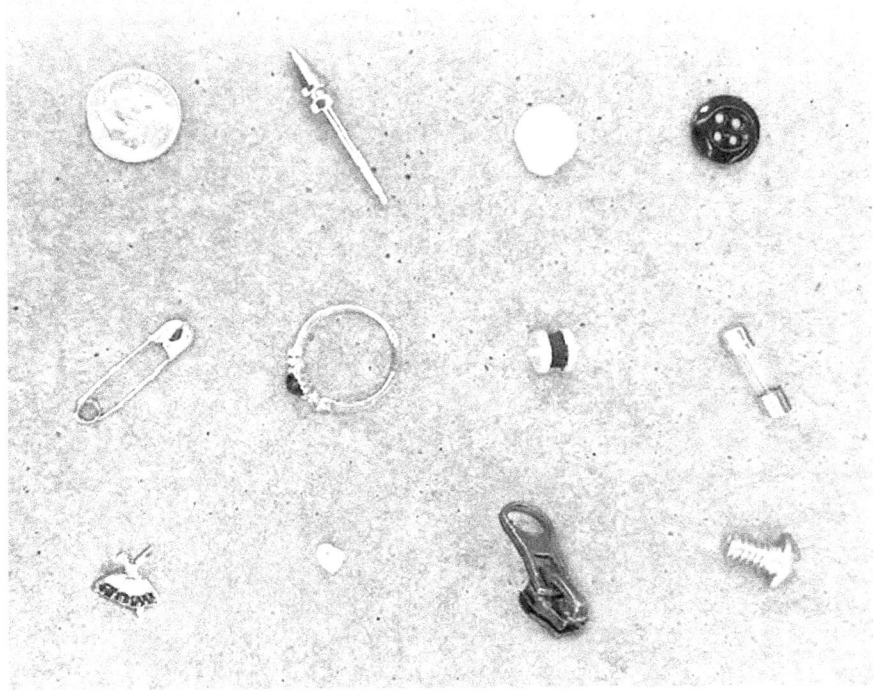

Bullet Cartridge Casing

9 mm diameter
24 mm length
brass
open on one end
interior empty

plucked from the lint drawer of a dryer at the laundromat by
    an attendant

but before,

slid through one of countless holes in the drum wall to the
    lint drawer below
eased out of the pocket into the load of clothes while
    tumbling in a hot dryer
submerged in the washer, solo, deep in a pocket
overlooked by probing fingers
warmed by human flesh next to some keys
lifted lightly through chilly air and tucked into right front
    jeans pocket
caressed by tufts of grass, looking shiny and foreign
ejected upward through a port, twirling then arcing downward
separated from its front partner, the bullet, which was
    propelled forward down a barrel
forced backward in the chamber by a massive explosion
    of gunpowder
pierced by a firing pin which ignited the primer
struck by a hammer
rested snug and content until a finger pressed a trigger
popped into a firearm chamber when the slide pulled back
shoved upward with companions into the handle of a gun
loaded following 9 others into a magazine

selected from available rounds
sat on truck gate under a box lid flapping in the breeze
bounced on a vehicle floorboard
jostled around in a thin, crinkly plastic bag
purchased with 49 others in the box for $24.99
placed on a smooth glass counter
lowered from a shelf by an employee in a colorful vest
resided in a thin cardboard box of ammo with black
  and red lettering
waited complete and whole: cartridge consisting of bullet,
  casing, gunpowder and primer.

Fear or Excitement or _____ generated a decision in
a human mind.   (Fill in the blank)

The Anatomy of a Cartridge

primer + propellant + casing + projectile (the bullet) = 1 cartridge
                                        or
                                   1 round
                              of ammunition

Possible Space Alien Gift

Best Strange Plastic Object (top)
and Other Contenders

Strange Plastic Object

[Space alien in hovering flying saucer thinks:]
place finally dark
no Earthlings
unique fluid behind glass observed in box earlier
is this place like human zoo to watch this fluid?
or human science experiment, eep eep [creature laughs]
    for body covering transformation?
I must investigate this substance
I will select box "8" but why vertical infinity symbol?

[Alien teleports into washer #8, and remotely starts it.]
splash
slap
swirl
swish

so this is Earth-prolific H2O
soft or hard dependent on velocity of motion
variable and wide temperature range in liquid form
I can eject gases from any of my 739 orifices to
    create bubbles in it
eeeowwwbbblubbharghoudaaahhmmaabaappaawoodoo!!
I like this Earth-prolific H2O
must report this finding back to my planet
but am confused with this place
why do humans come and go in their Earthly vehicles with
    so many body coverings and place them in this box?
inefficient
why not have body covering permanently attached to
    human body and simultaneously expose both to H2O?

[Alien teleports out of washer back to flying saucer and thinks:]
I may not return but have left precious gift to humans
emitted from orifice #442 [gratitude orifice] for my
    H2O experience

The next morning an attendant, while cleaning,
finds a strange plastic object in washer #8.

Toy Wars

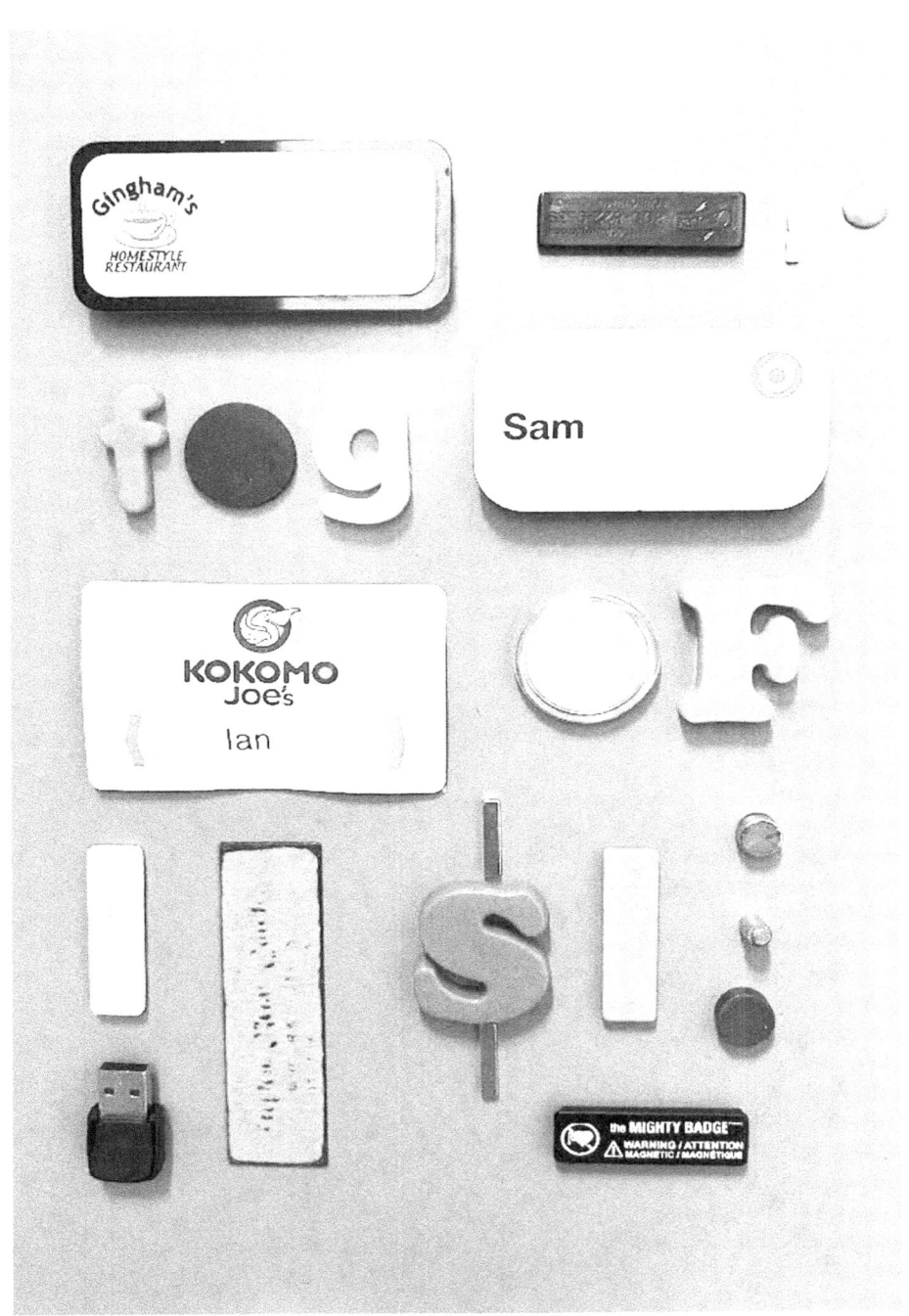

Magnetic Attraction

The Lighter Side

Chapter 6

America:
The Beautiful, the Blessed, the Beleaguered

Every citizen's perspective about their country is shaped by a list of factors: location and timing of birth, gender, race, socio-economic level, religion, family upbringing and more. I added business owner to my mix in 2018. I expected challenges in addition to anxieties over business debt and my back and knuckles surviving but never envisioned a pandemic, racial upheaval, massive inflation and more. I remain grateful, and hopeful for this amazing nation I love, but am concerned. In these final few poems I share my perspective on USA. Like a basket of laundry, perhaps full of dirty, worn but beloved items, it sits there, waiting for willing hands to tackle it.

My Own Sort of Rushmore

We spend time together,
us five,
though not enough,
in the office at the plastic table,
on the backside of the change machine
as I remove you and pour in quarters.

I ask questions and you four
from the messy stacks of bills I build,
sometime provide answers
despite your glances and stoic poses.
It's my own sort of Rushmore:
private
2D
muted shades of green and white paper.

Oh Hamilton, adorning the $10,
uber-productive statesman but our president not to be,
lover of words and this baby nation,
you were rapped into notoriety by another wordsmith, Miranda.
I follow your gaze from a handsome profile above a scarf
and search for the vision that impassioned you.

And on the $5,
President Lincoln, humble Abe,
your face sculpted by personal and national sorrows.
Our #16 whose term and life were squelched too soon.
A thinker, a writer, a rare soul who could see the long view.
Sir, what is the path to sew this divided country together?

Andrew Jackson, #7, least known to me.
I recall some rumblings to contest your spot on the $20
but per Wiki,
you were a fighter of big banks and for the common man.

I'm common.
so how can I best fight my fights?

George, premier patriot,
undisputed #1,
your impetus helped form this country.
On the lowly $1,
you are probably seen and handled the most.
Fitting.
Of the four comrades,
you're the only one to look me in the eye.
You can speak directly to me sir.
I'm listening.

The worn, the crisp, the well-traveled bills
that your four faces grace,
I wish by merely touching
I could gain all that you gained in your lifetimes.

You four nation builders,
please help me build my business,
strengthen me and my communities.

Make this money and my efforts multiply,
not for legacy,
not for greed,
but for goodness and rightness and abundance for many.

Our time is up.
I wrap rubber bands around you and your clones,
zip you up in the bank bag
and tuck you all into the dark cube of a safe
where protected,
you can rest undisturbed and prepare to share more wisdom
when we meet again.

"Made In"

Anyone can travel just by doing laundry.
Simply check the tags.

Stroke those thick Egyptian cotton sheets with high
thread count as you fold them and anticipate your
afternoon nap in their embrace after your camel ride.

Pair those nicely woven compression socks
and marvel at the massive nylon knitting looms
that birthed them in Taiwan with high tech precision
and efficiency.

Admire the beads and bling on a decorative pillow from India
as you remove it from a protective mesh washing bag
and place it to air dry on the folding rack, or rather
back onto a dusty shelf in a vendor's overflowing stall
on a bustling street shared by cars, motorcycles, bikes
and cows.

Spot treat with care that dark red splotch
on the Mexican tablecloth handwoven in bold colors
as you plan the next meal you'll be serving at your hacienda.
Chicken fajitas or mole sauce with pork?

Place those bright plaid krama, Cambodian scarves,
in the washer so they'll be clean and fresh
to protect your head and neck from the hot sun
when you explore the ruins of Ankor Wat.

Spread out that Shetland wool sweater from Scotland
to dry on the flat drying rack as you anticipate
the views of the North Sea on your next hike while wearing it.

BAND···N··· 14

Members Mark···
STANDARD
100% COTTON
MADE IN TURK···

···HENTIC
···BLISHED 1972

LADIE···
EXTRA LARGE/TG ···
···

100% EGYPTIAN
COTTON

Columbia
Sportswear Company®
PORTLAND OREGON U.S.A
L
MADE IN JORDAN
FABRIQUE EN JORDANIE

NINEWEST
JEANS
14
MADE IN
INDONESIA

ANOOTHI
MADE IN INDIA

Joseph A.
QU'EST-CE QUE C'EST SILK? ®
PARIS·LONDON·NEW YORK
L
67% SILK/SOIE
3% NYLON
0% SPANDEX
··· MADE IN U·S·A
···

continued

Gawk at the sheer volume of clothing, textiles and linens
from China,
jeans and shirts in array of styles,
light jackets and coats, fleece wear,
baby clothes, school uniforms,
canvas and poly sneakers,
tights, yoga pants, pleather slacks,
bras, slips and underwear in various makes and models,
nylon and cotton sportswear, bearing logos of US teams,
as overwhelmed,
you depart smog choked Beijing on a bullet train bound
for the glorious terracotta sculptures in Xi'an.

Gee, with all this traveling while I work at the laundromat
I'm probably going to be too exhausted
to go anywhere once I finally do retire.

But in all my wanderings
I question
why so few tags say "Made In USA?"

Say Their Names, Even While Doing Laundry

The author encourages this poem be read out loud, particularly the lines in quotations which are spoken by the human subject in this poem. The italics are what that subject is thinking.

Someday I'll have my own home with a washer and dryer.
But not yet.
So, I better head to the laundromat with all this dirty laundry.
There goes a few hours and 20 bucks, but it can't wait.
I'd rather get some real exercise but just don't have
the time with all the hours I work.
I know, I'll wear my running gear there and while my
    clothes wash
I'll jog through that neighborhood.
Finally got these machines loaded…I'm off.
"Run with me **Armaud Arbery**, run free, always."
Gotta push myself since I don't have much time.
I'm really sweating now and winded.
"These breaths are for you **Eric Garner**, **Derrick Scott** and **Manuel Ellis**.
And an extra-long one for **George Floyd**."
Phew, I better slow down.
Hey, are those kids in that park playing with sticks or
    toy guns or what?
"**Tamir Rice**, wherever you are, I hope you're playing with
    whatever you want to."
Think I'll head to the convenience store across the street
to buy a cold drink and snack.
Is that someone walking straight down the middle
    of the street?
"Oh, **Michael Brown**, what a new era you birthed in Ferguson."
My playlist is keeping me pumped through my headphones.
"I'm just going let that rhythm move my arms and feet,
in your honor **Elijah McClain**."
I don't care what anyone thinks.

continued

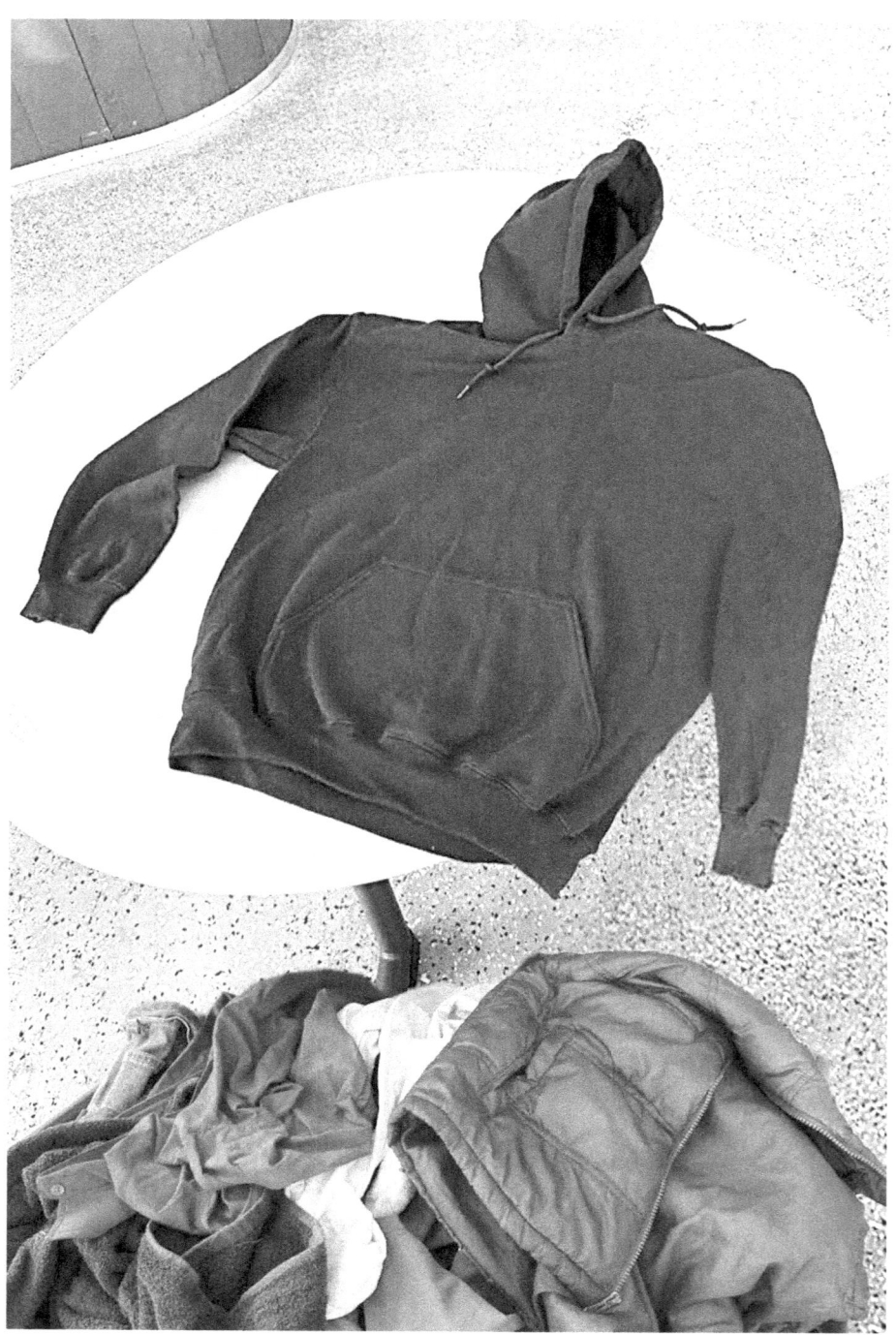

I feel good.

I'm alive.

Ok, time to shift my clothes to the dryer.

Maybe I'll sit out in my car now and listen to more music while I wait.

What's that customer in the next car saying about my music and me?

"There's still no shortage of intolerant people, right, **Jordan Davis***?"*

Ok, the dryer stopped. I'll just fold my clothes real quick.

Oops, this is still a little damp.

"Eh, **Trayvon Martin***, I love my hoodie, too."*

I'll just drape it over the top of the basket and head out.

Gosh it's dark. Not that many cars out tonight.

S#*@...I just rolled through that stop sign and there's a cop car under those trees.

"What are my chances **Philando Castile***,* **Walter Scott***,* **Sandra Bland***,* **Dante Wright** *and* **Tyre Nichols***?"*

Yay, I'm home.

Ugh, these baskets are heavy to drag upstairs.

I better put this all this stuff away right now or I'll just skip it.

What are those strange noises outside?

"Dare I peek out my window to investigate like **Atatiana Jefferson***?"*

Naw, I'm wiped.

Forget dinner, I just wanna crash.

Ah, clean pajamas and sheets.

I hope my sleep is deep and undisturbed.

"You know what I mean, **Breonna Taylor***, don't you, dear."*

May we all rest well.

"Say Their Names" Refresher [2]

Presented in order of appearance in the poem

Armaud Arbery
In Santilla Shores, GA on 2/23/20, while jogging through a neighborhood, this 25-year-old black man was followed by three white men in trucks suspecting Armaud of burglary who then cornered, assaulted, shot and killed him.

Eric Garner
In Staten Island, NY on 7/17/14 this 43-year-old black man was suspected of selling single cigarettes from a pack without the proper tax stamps by a NYPD officer, who used a chokehold to wrestle Eric to the ground during the arrest. Eric said "I can't breathe" 11 times while being pinned down by several officers, lost consciousness and was pronounced dead at the hospital one-hour later.

Derrick Scott
In Oklahoma City, OK on 5/20/19 this 42-year-old-black man was reported brandishing a firearm. During the arrest, Derrick ran from police, was chased and a loaded handgun removed from his pocket as he was subdued. When pinned down by police, Derrick repeatedly said, "I can't breathe" and asked for his medicine. He was DOA.

Manuel Ellis
In Tacoma, WA on 3/3/20 this 33-year-old black man, deemed suspicious, was stopped by police while walking home from a convenience store. Police and witnesses provided conflicting stories on the cause for arrest during which multiple officers used chokeholds, punching, tasers, restraints and a hood to control him. Despite saying "I can't breathe" during a prolonged struggle Manuel died at the scene after CPR attempts.

George Floyd

In Minneapolis, MN on 5/25/20 this 46-year-old black man was arrested for suspected $20 counterfeit bill use at a grocery store. The responding four officers forcibly removed George from his car and handcuffed him. When they attempted to put him in the squad car, a struggle ensued, as George stiffened and dropped to the ground stating he was claustrophobic. One officer placed his knee on George's neck for 9 minutes and 29 seconds to subdue him while the other three officers watched and prevented any intervention from bystanders. George said "I can't breathe" over 20 times and cried out to his mother. He gradually became silent, motionless and pulseless. He was taken to the hospital and pronounced dead one hour later, eventually ruled from cardiopulmonary arrest due to asphyxiation from neck compression and restraint. His murder sparked an eruption of protests against police brutality on nonwhites and minorities worldwide.

Tamir Rice

In Cleveland, OH on 11/22/14, this 12-year-old black youth who was playing with a replica toy gun under a rec center pavilion was shot by a police officer. The officer was responding to a dispatch call about an armed male while the initial phone call was about a "juvenile" and "probably harmless" gun. Tamir was shot almost immediately upon the officers' arrival as it was suspected he was drawing his gun. He died of his injuries the next day.

Michael Brown

In Ferguson, MO on 8/9/14, this 18-year-old black man and a friend were stopped by an officer patrolling in his car for walking down the middle of a street. The pair were suspect-ed of robbery and assault at a nearby convenience store. During the verbal and physical exchange, the officer shot Michael in the right hand from inside the car and another six times in the front of his body during the ensuing foot chase.

continued

Michael died at the scene. The incident gave rise to "Hands Up, Don't Shoot" slogan and gesture, despite accounts Michael charged the officer without surrendering. In response, waves of violent protests ("Ferguson Riots") with looting, destruction and fires erupted along with peaceful counter protests and marches over a span of months necessitating nightly curfews and National Guard involvement.

Elijah McClain
In Aurora, CO on 8/24/19 this 23-year-old black man was stopped while walking home from a convenience store for being reported "sketchy but harmless" as wearing a ski mask and flailing his arms, possibly dancing to music. During his forcible arrest and being pinned down, Elijah vomited, apologized for squirming and stated, "I just can't breathe correctly." After paramedics injected him with 500mg of the sedative ketamine, excessive for his size, Elijah went into cardiac arrest and became brain dead. Life support was removed and 3 days later he died.

Jordan Davis
In Jacksonville, FL on 11/23/12 the 17-year-old black high school student was shot to death in back seat of a car in front of a gas station convenience store by a white man, parked next to Jordan's, during an argument over loud music played by Jordan and three friends in their car.

Trayvon Martin
In Sanford, FL on 2/26/12, this 17-year-old black high school student who was staying with relatives (his father's fiancé) in a gated community, was shot and killed by the neighborhood watch coordinator. Trayvon, wearing a dark hoodie, was returning from a convenience store to buy snacks. Due to multiple break-ins at the community, the watchman, suspecting foul play, followed Trayvon. There was a struggle during which Trayvon was shot and killed. The watchman claimed self-defense giving attention to the "Stand-Your-Ground" law.

Philando Castile
In Falcon Heights, MN on 7/6/16, this 32-year-old black man was killed during a traffic stop by police suspecting him of favoring a robber. In the car was also Philando's girlfriend, who videotaped the incident on her cell phone, and her young daughter. As Philando provided his driver's license, he informed the cop he had a gun. The cop accused Philando of reaching for his weapon, contradicted by the girlfriend and video footage, and shot Philando point blank five times. He died 20 minutes later at the hospital.

Walter Scott
In North Charleston, SC on 4/4/15, this 50-year-old black man was pulled over for a nonfunctioning brake light. Walter fled from the car and during the foot chase and struggle,was tased and fatally shot five times in the back by the officer.

Sandra Bland
In Prairie View, TX on 7/10/15, this 28-year-old black women was pulled over for failing to signal a lane change. The exchange with the officer escalated. He demanded she put out her cigarette, tried to pull her out of the car and threatened to tase her. Sandra was arrested and while awaiting bond, was found hanged to death in her jail cell three days later.

Daunte Wright
In Brooklyn Center, MN on 4/11/21, this 20-year-old black man was pulled over for a signaling violation, expired license tags and an air freshener hanging from rearview mirror (against the law in MN) by a trainee cop. Daunte did not have a driver's license or proof of insurance. The cop ran his name and learned he had open warrant for his arrest, and attempted to arrest him but Daunte, initially compliant and standing next to the car, began resisting and stepped back in the car. The supervising officer interceded and yelled "Taser!" but instead drew her handgun and shot Daunte once in the chest as he drove away. The car crashed shortly ahead and Daunte died at the scene.

continued

Tyre Nichols

In Memphis, TN on 1/7/23, this 29-year-old black man was stopped allegedly for reckless driving. He was pulled from the car, there was a struggle and Tyre broke loose. He was chased, caught and then multiple officers viciously beat Tyre for three minutes also using pepper spray, stun gun and baton. Tyre died of his injuries 3 days later.

Atatiana Jefferson

In Fort Worth, TX on 10/12/19, this 28-year-old black woman was playing video games with her 8-year-old nephew when she heard noises in the backyard. Officers were investigating the backyard with flashlights in response to a neighbor's non-emergency call about an open front door at her home in the early morning hours. Officers called out "Put your hands up! Show me your hands!" then shot and killed Atatiana as she looked out from her window.

Breonna Taylor

In Louisville, KY, this 26-year-old black women on 3/13/20, was shot in her apartment during a "no-knock" search warrant by seven officers as part of a late night, drug dealing investigation. Suspecting intruders, Breonna's boyfriend shot at the officers, and in the ensuing gunfire, Breonna was hit six times and died at the scene.

[2]Information here was gleaned from various internet sources, including Wikipedia, YouTube, newspaper and TV clips. The author aims to present as accurate and unbiased information as possible hoping readers will do deeper dives. Many of these cases included confusing details (e.g., conflicting witnesses, multiple autopsies) and involved perfect storms of tragedies such as miscommunications relays, stress and short time frames. And sadly, most happened against a backdrop of racial profiling or in communities of economic imbalance. This is short list of names. And the bottom line: there is inequity in America. May we all think, pray, speak and act towards a time of no lists and when fairness and justice truly exist for all of us.

The Statue and Us

I get to know some customers,
about their physical bodies and their stories.

A woman tries to quickly fold clothes overflowing from
a big dryer.
She coaches a child doing homework at the next table,
disciplines a rowdy toddler and watches an infant in a
carrier at her feet.
"My neck and back are killing me," she says as she
stretches for a brief break.

With a shopping cart, the older man brings in his laundry.
His sneakers are worn down on the outer edges due to
crooked legs since he doesn't drive and walks everywhere.
A housekeeper at an understaffed nursing home, weary but
always cheerful.

Another customer, very short, with bad rotator cuffs has us
iron for her.
She misses it, joking it likely helped wear her shoulders out.
"What will I be able to do in retirement?" she wonders.

I cross my fingers that the guy with diabetic foot drop
doesn't trip as he awkwardly steers a wheeled cart.
I know better to offer help as he puts quarters in the machine
even though the neuropathy in his hands limits his dexterity.

"All I could do while driving was eat," admits the trucker
transformed by gastric bypass surgery in Mexico.
Now 100# lighter, he ponders how to deal
with sagging skin and bone on bone knee arthritis.

continued

The husband pretends to let his amputee wife in a
wheelchair take charge.
A daughter keeps her senile mother safely nearby in a chair.
The disabled girlfriend and boyfriend work as a team.
A whistle still attached to shirt in a dirty load signals
someone's dependence.
So many caregivers and receivers doing laundry at our mat.
Their faces display degrees of acceptance and fatigue.

And lots of braces ride in on customers.
Back braces, wrist braces, slings,
pull on neoprene and elaborate hinged knee braces of
many varieties.
All lashed on to support ailing body parts.

Related to that, I see lots of waddlers and limpers here.
I worry the automatic door won't stay open long enough.

Plus, folks with twitches, head bobbles, twisted fingers,
scars, bad or no teeth.

As my own body also surrenders to time and use,
I feel for them all.
Actually, they're my peeps.

The working class.
The hardy, hardworking souls
who plod and persevere.

Not CEOs checking portfolios,
bejeweled professional athletes,
lacquered real estate agents or
the constant stream of TV entertainers.
Nope.

We are foreigners in each other's worlds.
Not that I begrudge these gazillionaires their material wealth,
it's just that they haven't been honed by physical hardship,
lack of resources or opportunities,
long patches of no health insurance,
a depressing apartment, crappy job or
just outright bad luck or timing or both.

I think of that tall stalwart Statue of Liberty
holding the torch high to welcome all immigrants
and spur us blessed Americans
to work and strive for freedom and equality.
What if we took her statue-ness away?

Would she only hold that torch at chest height
or perhaps need both hands?
Would she have a forward head and furrowed brow?
Maybe she'd have some stubborn belly fat from stress,
postmenopausal poor sleep
or a wee bit too much alcohol?
If she lifted up her copper robe
would it reveal her cock-eyed knees,
varicose veins, bunions?

What would she say if she'd walked this path of daily
existence and witnessed her fellow humans battling
hardship after hardship?
"Hang in there?"
No, too trite.

I'd like to think it's this:

"I'm not lighting the way for you.
I need it to watch and learn from you."

Book Discussion Questions

A. **GENERATE GENERAL DISCUSSION** about the book. What did you enjoy/not enjoy about it? What were the main themes? Did any specific poems or the book collectively address the issue of career pivot? How did the experiences of the laundromat in the book compare to your own (if you've ever gone)? How will it impact your future visits?

B. **CONSIDER POETRY**. In appreciating the flexibility of poetry and its core elements (rhyme, rhythm, sound devices, figurative language, form) how effective were/were not these free verse poems in sharing the topics in the book? Would rhyming poems or another literary genre (e.g., short story, essay, memoir, etc.) have worked better or not? Were readers drawn to any specific poems and what emotions were evoked?

C. **Ch 1 EXAMINE THINGS** at the laundromat. What were some surprising objects and how were poems used to share their essence or value to the author? Consider if/how noticing and appreciating things cultivates contentment.

D. **Ch 2 Similarly, EXAMINE TASKS** done at the mat. Which poems revealed details on expected tasks versus some unusual tasks? Explain how the author found beauty in the mundane and if/how we can do this in all realms of our daily lives. If there are readers in the group that are also business owners or involved in Human Relations, discuss if/how the comparison of Sisyphus in "Staffing Woes" likens to their staffing experiences.

E. **Ch 3 MEET CUSTOMERS.** Which were your favorite customer-poems? How were their attributes developed? How effective was the use of repetition as a writing technique in some poems ("Big Jim", "Julia", and "Our Secret")? What were the reactions of cat lovers in the group to "Cathy, the Cat Lady"?

F. **Ch 4 TALK ABOUT TALKERS.** Similes, which use like or as, compared the talking habits of customers to various things or actions in the mat. For example: "Like the water gushing into the washer...you gush forth at me..." Did you find the comparisons and enjoy them or not? Were the strategies on how to handle the different type of talkers helpful, and if so, how? Did you recognize yourself or someone else as a specific type of talker?

G. **Ch 5 PLAY WITH DETRITUS!** Discuss the word "detritus" and if it best captures the odds and ends found at the mat. What were your reactions to the fictional backstory poems: amazement, disbelief, humor or what? Can detritus in your life, from a junk drawer, car floorboard, purse or wherever, inspire a poem?

H. **Ch 6 PONDER PERSPECTIVE.** How has being a business owner impacted the author's perspective on money and the economy, racial discrimination or the American Dream? Did you read "Say their Names" out loud and use the "Refresher"? Does the final short chapter encourage readers to be optimistic and take action or too cynical and give up hope?

Additional BONUS MATERIAL available at:
www.leahmschulte.com

www.ingramcontent.com/pod-product-compliance
Lightning Source LLC
Chambersburg PA
CBHW060542130626
46553CB00002B/871